MLA Made Easy

Citation Basics for Beginners

Marilyn Heath

A LINWORTH PUBLISHING BOOK

LIBRARIES UNLIMITED
An Imprint of ABC-CLIO, LLC

A B C ☗ C L I O

Santa Barbara, California • Denver, Colorado • Oxford, England

Copyright 2010 by Linworth Publishing

Library of Congress Cataloging-in-Publication Data

Heath, Marilyn.
  MLA made easy : citation basics for beginners / Marilyn Heath.
    p. cm.
  Includes bibliographical references and index.
  ISBN 978-1-58683-343-5 (pbk. : acid-free paper)
  1. Bibliographical citations—Handbooks, manuals, etc.
2. MLA handbook for writers of research papers—Handbooks,
manuals, etc.   I. Title.
  PN171.F56H43   2010
  808'.02—dc22   2009015280

ISBN 978-1-58683-343-5
EISBN 978-1-58683-409-8

14   13   12   11   10   1   2   3   4   5

This book is also available on the World Wide Web as an eBook.
Visit www.abc-clio.com for details.

ABC-CLIO, LLC
130 Cremona Drive, P.O. Box 1911
Santa Barbara, California 93116-1911

This book is printed on acid-free paper (∞)
Manufactured in the United States of America

Table of Contents

PART II: PARENTHETICAL DOCUMENTATION

PART III: FORMATTING

Table of Figures

Acknowledgments

I would like to thank all those who helped make this book possible. My supportive editing team, Kate Vande Brake and Cynthia Anderson at Linworth Publishing, believed in this project before I was sure myself. A special thank-you to all of the many generous authors, publishers, and artists who made their work available to me so this book could become a reality.

About the Author

Marilyn Heath has been a teacher and teacher-librarian for more than 20 years. She has worked with students from middle school through graduate school and enjoys them all. She earned her MLIS from the University of South Carolina in 1989 and an Ed.D. in Educational Leadership with a major in Curriculum and Instruction in 1999. She achieved National Board certification in 2003. Over the years, she has written lots of research papers and guided countless students as they wrote theirs.

Marilyn is a frequent presenter at state and national conferences on a variety of topics. Her first book, *Electronic Portfolios: A Guide to Professional Development and Assessment* (Linworth, 2004), was selected as the Association of Educational Publishers 2005 winner of the Distinguished Achievement Award for a professional development book.

Marilyn has one grown son, Michael, and three very spoiled cats. In her spare time, she teaches online classes, reads, gardens, and works on redecorating her townhouse. She lives and works in Greenville, South Carolina.

Introduction: Getting Ready to Cite

Reading books, Web sites, databases, and other sources of information for research is different from any other kind of reading. The purpose of reading for research is to pull together information from several sources and then evaluate, analyze, or synthesize it to create something original. While conducting research, students read for both information and understanding. They often skim and scan multiple sources to find answers to research questions. Student researchers might find an idea in one book, use it with some data from a reference book, and then incorporate some information from a Web site to construct a persuasive argument, analyze cause and effect, or create a unique story, piece of art, Web page, or brochure.

When students conduct research, they should be using information from several sources to create something new. Their creations reflect their own ideas, findings, or opinions, depending upon the assignment. This is how research differs from simply writing a report: Instead of just "reporting back" the information they find, students use the information they find to reach conclusions, justify opinions, or formulate original ideas. The illustration in Figure FM.1 is a simplified model of the critical thinking processes students use when they create a research project.

Rarely do students read a source from beginning to end when they are using information in this way. Often, they skim or scan the material, looking for the information they need. In an encyclopedia or reference book, especially, student researchers use only a very small part of the whole book or set of books, because they are looking for answers to research questions that the teacher has asked or that the students have generated themselves. If the media specialist and teacher are using the BigSix research model (Berkowitz and Eisenberg), then the students probably thought of these questions as they were completing Step #1: "What information will I need to complete my task?"

However, students often find that the questions they or their teacher pose lead to other questions not originally considered. Questions lead to more questions, and the pursuit of answers leads students to more sources. Rarely do students find all the information to completely answer their research questions in one source. Using several sources of information also helps ensure that research questions are answered completely and accurately and that various perspectives and multiple ideas are considered.

The Student Research Process

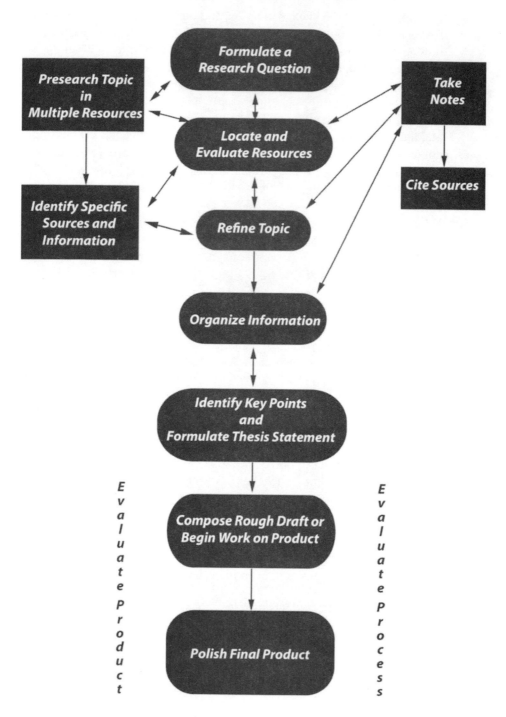

Figure FM.1. The student research process.

This inquiry-based approach to student research is consistent with standards included in many of the content areas, especially social studies, science, and English language arts. For example, standard 7 of the NCTE/IRA Standards for the English Language Arts states, in part, that students "generate ideas and questions" and that they "gather, evaluate, and synthesize data from a variety of sources...to communicate their discoveries in ways that suit their purpose and audience" (NCTE). Mathematics, social studies, and science also address the importance of inquiry-based learning and the value of students' abilities to evaluate, analyze, synthesize, problem-solve, and communicate findings and conclusions.

Recognizing the importance of the inquiry-based approach and the accompanying student skills, the American Association of School Librarians (AASL) has published *Standards for the 21st-Century Learner,* a document that addresses the dispositions students need for the knowledge-based society in which they will live and work. According to AASL, students must be able to:

- Inquire, think critically, and gain knowledge
- Draw conclusions, make informed decisions, apply knowledge to new situations, and create new knowledge
- Share knowledge and participate ethically and productively as members of our democratic society
- Pursue personal and aesthetic growth (AASL).

By the time student researchers have accumulated all the information they need for their research projects, they may have a wide variety of sources. Each source that they use for the assignment has to be cited before the final product is complete. It is imperative that they let their readers know where they found the facts and information that they have included in their final project. Sources may include books, magazines, journals, newspapers, videos and television programs, works of art, Internet sites, databases, and even interviews, blogs, and wikis.

For each source that students use, they must write a citation that shows readers where they found the information. Sometimes teachers tell students that it is permissible to submit just a list of titles and authors or Web sites with no other documenting information. Usually this is done in an attempt to make documentation easier for students or because the teacher does not really understand or appreciate the importance of correct citations. Such a strategy does a disservice to all involved. It sends a message to students that giving proper credit to others is not terribly important; it promotes haphazard research and, by doing so, undermines the assignment. Ultimately, such an approach can do more harm than that.

Some educators have suggested that, as our society becomes increasingly dependent upon knowledge, the focus on citation format is slightly archaic. We should be teaching children the ability to ask perceptive questions and to solve problems, the ability to think creatively, and the ability to develop and communicate new knowledge. Agreed. It is my contention, however, that as the focus on knowledge creation and sharing increases, the importance of correct citation creation increases, as well. The successful creation and communication of new knowledge depends upon the ethical use of information. Recognizing where information came from and giving proper credit is not elective; it is essential. Anyone who has turned to a Works Cited page to find where an author got his or her information knows how important correct citations can be. The ability to trace ideas and information back to their original sources is imperative in a knowledge-based society.

"High expectations" is a term educators have used for years, and it should apply to every research assignment. Often, however, teachers who are themselves unsure of citation writing or who dislike research shy away from using the media center or assigning research to their students. National standards, however, indicate that aversion to research should not be an option. Media specialists and the skills they can help students learn are more critical now than at any other time.

This manual can help teachers and media specialists alike as they work with student researchers. Not only does it include clear, precise instructions for creating citations in MLA format, but also it helps everyone involved understand the importance of creating accurate, complete citations for every source used in the research process.

MLA Style

During the years students spend in school, they may hear of or even be asked to use different types of citation formats. MLA and APA are two of the most frequently used, but most high schools use the MLA format (Knowledge Base). MLA stands for the Modern Language Association of America. The Association's purpose in publishing the *Handbook for Writers of Research Papers,* now in its seventh edition, is to give students a common convention that directs readers to the sources they have used in their research (xiii). The handbook is designed as a guide for high school and college students, but sometimes students who are beginning research find it difficult to use. Further, many teachers and media specialists are starting to introduce citations to students in the upper elementary grades and in middle school. The *MLA Handbook* was never intended for younger students, so media specialists and teachers have not had a resource to help them.

The purpose of this guide is to make documentation easy for beginning researchers. Whether a student is in middle school or a college freshman, if he is new to the idea of citations, he may find the rules and formats confusing. This guide helps media specialists and teachers as they work with students who are learning how to document their sources. Clear explanations and examples illustrate citations for the Works Cited page, and a chapter on parenthetical documentation explains how to include the necessary citations within their writing.

A word of caution is in order. Users of this handbook may note that, at times, citation formats varies slightly from that given in the *MLA Handbook*. Discrepancies occur because MLA occasionally requires or recommends more data in citations than are necessary to adequately identify a source of information. Here is an example: The *MLA Handbook* tells users that, if a book has previously been published as a hardcover edition but the writer is using a paperback edition, then the citation should include the date of the hardcover edition before the publication information of the paperback (171). In other words, the citation should state:

Smith, John. *An MLA Adventure.* 2006. New York: Acme, 2008. Print.

In this instance, 2006 is the copyright date of the hardcover edition. I see no reason to include the date of the hardcover edition, since it does not help the reader find the same source that the writer used. True, the two editions are essentially the same book, but the page numbers probably differ. Therefore, I would write the citation omitting that piece of information:

Smith, John. *An MLA Adventure.* New York: Acme, 2008. Print.

This citation does what a citation is intended to do: It gives credit to the appropriate author for the information used, and it leads the reader to the exact source that the researcher cited. Knowing that there is an earlier hardcover edition might by helpful to someone, but it does not lead the reader to the same information the researcher used. Further, the reader would have to know what the additional date meant. Otherwise, the date is just an extraneous piece of information that can lead to confusion for both the citation writer and the reader. As students progress (or as teachers require), they can graduate to the *MLA Handbook* and include this or other citation elements as necessary.

Another example is in order, since it illustrates one of the changes apparent in the seventh edition of the handbook. In the past, the name of the series that a book is part of has been an integral part of a citation. In the new edition, the name of the series is still required, but it is now placed at the end of the citation. This placement seems awkward and makes the series name appear to be extraneous information. Since it usually is extraneous information, I have simply omitted the series designation in the citations in this book.

This guide concentrates on the two chapters of the *MLA Handbook* that are used the most, the chapters on documentation. Chapter Five addresses "Documentation: Preparing the List of Works Cited," and Chapter Six covers "Documentation: Citing Sources in the Text." All formats are taken from the seventh edition of the *MLA Handbook* and should apply to most citation situations.

Having said that, it should also be noted that anyone who has any experience with citations knows how easy it is to come across a source that does not seem to fit any example given. That would be true no matter how exhaustive the citation guide. In order to keep this guide brief and easy to use, not every contingency is covered here. If a question remains unanswered after consulting this guide, it is always a good idea to consult the latest edition of the *MLA Handbook*. If a question still remains, consider the two guiding principles for a citation: giving credit to the author or creator of the work, and leading the reader to the same source. Then decide upon a format, and use it consistently.

Contents and Organization

This book is based on the premise that citation construction is not difficult. Success depends upon understanding the logic of citations and ensuring that all citations answer three or four questions—the same questions for every type of citation, in the same order, every time (Figure FM.2). It is imperative that novice researchers be taught to find the answers to these questions. If they do not know how to do this, they will most certainly have problems constructing citations.

This book is divided into three parts. Part I explains how to create citations for the Works Cited page. Part II deals with parenthetical documentation, and Part III covers creating the Works Cited page and formatting the paper.

Who wrote the information used?   The author gets first mention in a citation.

What did the author write?   The title of the author's piece comes next.

Where is the piece found?   This information is necessary for every piece found in a larger work (e.g., a poem in a book or an article in a magazine or reference book, or a page of a Web site).

How was it published?   The answer must include the city, publisher, and copyright year if citing a book. All citations conclude with the source's format.

Figure FM.2. Citation creation questions. Answer these questions in order to create a correct citation.

Chapter One explains the three criteria for successful student research: understanding plagiarism, engaging research assignments, and the practice of research skills.

Chapter Two examines what information is necessary to create an MLA citation, where to find that information, and how to use the information to create citations. The guiding questions for creating citations are explained fully. This chapter also gives an overview of the basic reasons why citations are important.

Chapter Three explains how to cite all types of books. The chapter is subdivided into two parts: citations for books by authors and citations for edited books. There are extensive examples of books with multiple authors, reference books, including encyclopedias, multivolume sets, and books in a series. Each example includes a facsimile of a book's title page with helpful inserts that identify each piece of information found there, followed by citations of the examples.

Chapter Four follows the same format as the preceding chapter by explaining citations for various magazines, journals, and newspapers. Weekly and monthly publications are examined, as are unique features of periodical citations. Again, facsimiles of the publications, accompanied by explanatory inserts, are included with citations for the examples.

Chapter Five explains how to cite Web sites, databases, and all other computer sources. This chapter follows the same format as the previous two.

Chapter Six covers citations for other, miscellaneous sources, such as videos, artwork, interviews, films, speeches, and performances.

Chapter Seven begins the second part of the book. It explains, with examples, how to incorporate the work of another without plagiarizing by using the techniques of summarizing, paraphrasing, and quoting.

Chapter Eight deals with parenthetical documentation. It focuses on the two main factors for writers to consider: accuracy and readability. Detailed guidelines are included.

The final section of the book begins with Chapter Nine, which explains the organization and formatting guidelines that must be followed when constructing the Works Cited page. It includes a sample Works Cited page.

The final chapter gives detailed instructions for formatting the paper as a whole, including page margins, headers, spacing, and indents. It includes instructions for setting up the paper in MS Word '97, Word 2003, and Word 2007.

Appendixes A through D include examples of every type of information source covered in this book, along with the correct citation and helpful guidelines. Appendix E includes templates that can help students understand the various types of citations and give them practice constructing citations. Appendix F includes suggested teaching activities.

PART ONE

Understanding and Creating MLA Citations

CHAPTER ONE

Research without Plagiarism

Plagiarism has become the bane of teachers and media specialists as they work with student researchers. The problem ranges from the blatancy of buying papers online to the "cut and paste" method employed by students from middle school through college. Sometimes students claim not to know that what they are doing is wrong. Sometimes they might be telling the truth.

A student can plagiarize many ways. Some common examples include:

- Turning in a research paper written by someone else—many Web sites offer research papers for sale or offer to write a research paper for a fee
- Copying and pasting text or pictures from a Web site into a research paper without citations
- Copying notes from a print source without a citation
- Including quotations and paraphrases in a research paper that are not cited
- Using factual information without citations
- Using artwork or photography from a Web site without a citation
- Using an artist's lyrics or music without a citation

Plagiarism is a serious problem in schools. In elementary school, students may be allowed to copy information from encyclopedias or other sources and turn it in as "research." However, it is not research—it is plagiarism. As students get older and advance through school, the penalties for plagiarism become severe. In some high schools and colleges, students may fail a paper, fail a class, or even be expelled for plagiarism. Several colleges and university now give students who plagiarize a grade of "XF" in the class so that everyone who sees their transcripts will know they cheated by plagiarizing (Hollingsworth).

Some schools take a proactive approach to plagiarism and other forms of cheating by instituting an honor code or policy among students. Typically, students sign a statement that they have not cheated on a test or that they have not copied a paper. A reactive approach that other schools have employed is the use of plagiarism detection software. Programs such as Turnitin.com, CheckForPlagiarism.net, and others compare student work against databases of texts and generate a report based upon similarities.

Neither approach is foolproof, of course. Proponents of each express problems and concerns. Either strategy could be even more effective if it were used in conjunction with instruction on the ethical use of information. Students have to know what plagiarism is, why they should not engage in plagiarism, and what their alternatives are in order for any approach to produce the desired results.

The problem of plagiarism seems to be exacerbated by three conditions that often work in tandem. If one of them exists, plagiarism is likely. If all three exist, it is almost a certainty. They are the failure of teachers and media specialists to teach what plagiarism is; the failure of teachers and media specialists to collaboratively plan research that is engaging and requires critical thinking; and the failure of teachers and media specialists to teach the skills necessary for successful research.

Teaching Plagiarism

What is plagiarism, and how do we teach what it is? Simply put, plagiarism is presenting the work of someone else as our own. Whether a student copies a paragraph from a reference book, uses a chart from a Web site, or draws his own version of a well-known anime figure, the result is the same: The student has plagiarized if he does not give proper credit to the originator of the creation.

Too often, instruction boils down to the directive "Don't copy." However, in today's world of online, pirated music, movies, and video games, students often don't "get it" or don't care when teachers tell them that copying is wrong. It is a mistake to think that students will not plagiarize because they have been told not to or because it is wrong. When confronted, students often respond with a shrug, as if to say, "So what?" Copying and representing the information as your own, it seems, is just not a big deal.

What teachers and media specialists can do is to begin by teaching students the basics about plagiarism and copyright. A good place to start is with Carol Simpson's "Copyright and Plagiarism Guidelines for Students," found at her Web site, http://www.carolsimpson.com. It is an easy-to-read, one-page summary of what students can and cannot do.

Another important approach is to teach students alternatives to copying. In fact, they can teach students that it is okay to copy—if it is done correctly. They can teach students the skills of using quotations, paraphrasing, and summarizing. If students have ample experience using these three devices in smaller activities and assignments before they begin research, they will be able to apply them skillfully and knowledgeably as they conduct their research. They will already know how to use the work of another person without plagiarizing.

Engaging Research

To many students, the term "engaging research" sounds like an oxymoron. They think of research as an activity that forces them to find and then read material that is boring, hard to understand, and totally uninteresting. The result is an uninspired final product (often plagiarized) that leaves teachers shaking their heads and students sullen over another mediocre or failing grade.

It does not have to be that way. National content standards include inquiry-based problem-solving, the study of real-world problems and issues, and information finding using a variety of sources. With a world of topics to address and a wider variety of information sources than ever before, research can be engaging, interesting, and even fun.

The crucial piece that must be included in any research assignment is critical thinking. Too often, however, research projects stop at fact-finding. Consider this example: A science teacher announces that the class is going to the media center to "do research." The assignment is to select a disease from the list he has prepared and answer the following questions:

Who is likely to get the disease?

What are the symptoms of the disease?

How is the disease treated?

What is the prognosis for a person with the disease?

If the disease can be fatal, what is the mortality rate?

Students are to present their "findings" in a brochure they make in Microsoft Publisher. During their time in the media center, the teacher has a hard time keeping students on task, and discipline is an issue.

This is a worksheet assignment. No matter what the final product is, students are involved in doing nothing more than finding information and copying. It involves no critical thinking skills. Further, it does nothing to relate the information to real-world problems or solutions.

To truly be researchers, students must take the information they find and use it to construct their own knowledge. They should use it in ways that make them think, question, analyze, evaluate, compare, contrast—ways that involve critical thinking skills. The idea is to make the information-finding meaningful because it has a purpose. Recently a group of students at a local elementary school came up with an idea to help lower the cost of operating the school facility. They conducted research, used their findings to formulate a plan, and presented it to the school board. The district is now considering the feasibility of implementing the students' plan.

Taking research beyond the "reporting" stage helps reduce plagiarism because students must craft their own conclusions from the information they find. "So what?" is a great question to ask in order to get to critical thinking because there are so many places the question can go. So are questions that begin with "What if?" Think of the disease assignment and all the possibilities for meaningful research if students were given the opportunity to use the facts they found and to apply them to meaningful, thought-provoking questions. Too often, however, the fact-finding is the beginning and end of the assignment when it should be just the beginning of creative, constructive thinking.

In order for teachers to successfully create such thought-provoking research assignments, they should work closely with their media specialists. Teachers should think of the media specialist as the "research specialist" because that is what she is. Not only has she been formally trained in research, but also she is the person who knows what resources are available—not only in the school's media center but also in other local libraries, in the community, and on the Web. It is her job to make sure that every research assignment is successful for both teacher and students. The only way she can do that is to be involved from the inception of the project. Often, she can offer suggestions and strategies that the teacher may not have considered. She is trained to collaborate, and collaboration is part of her professional responsibilities. That said, she cannot make a poorly designed assignment work well if her only contribution is to reserve library time and pull books.

Teachers and media specialists do not have to work alone, however. National, state, and local resources are available in all content areas to help educators create well-crafted assignments. In addition, many Web resources, such as *Kathy Schrock's Guide for Educators* on Discovery Education's Web site, offer helpful information and creative ideas. Print resources, such as *Ban Those Bird Units! 15 Models for Teaching and Learning in Information-Rich and Technology-Rich Environments* by David Loertscher, Toni Buzzeo's books on collaboration, and books on inquiry-based learning, such as *Inquiry Learning through Librarian-Teacher Partnerships* by Violet H. Harada and Joan M. Yoshina, and *Inquiry-Based Learning* by Jean Donham et al., are just a few of the many resources that can help teachers and media specialists create projects that engage student researchers.

Research Skills

One of the biggest stumbling blocks to successful research is students' lack of research skills. Often students copy from books or cut and paste at the computer because they do not have the skills to do anything else. Research requires a set of discrete skills that many young people have not mastered. Research skills, like any other skills, must be practiced on a regular basis for students to improve.

Interestingly enough, many teachers do not think of these skills as part of the research process. For example, thinking of key words and synonyms is crucial to finding information from a book's index. Skimming and scanning are essential reading skills. So is identifying the main idea and supporting details. Knowing how to take notes is an obvious necessity, but no less important are more sophisticated skills such as evaluating Web sites and knowing how to use online databases. Of course students should already know how to summarize and paraphrase.

Many teachers believe that it is the job of the school's English or Language Arts teachers to teach these skills. They sometimes assume that students come to their classes already knowing how to do these things and are "research ready." Such assumptions are partially false. Yes, English teachers do teach these skills and many more. However, if the skills are not reinforced in other subjects by other teachers, students will not get the practice they need.

Further, teachers have different ways of doing things. Taking notes, for example, might look four different ways in four different classes. What is "vocabulary" in one class may be "focus words" in another and "key terms" in another. It behooves teachers and media specialists to make a scope and sequence of research skills so that all teachers in the school know what skills to reinforce at various grade levels, how to talk about them, and how they should be taught. Doing this would go a long way toward improving student research.

CHAPTER TWO

Understanding MLA Citations

Creating accurate MLA citations can be easy. All it involves, really, is knowing what information to include and where to find it and arranging it in the correct order with the correct punctuation. The *MLA Handbook for Writers of Research Papers* (7th ed.) lists citation elements in the order they usually appear in various types of citations. Understanding what elements need to be included in citations by answering the citation creation questions is a good way of ensuring that citations are creating correctly.

Guidelines for Creating Citations

Figure 2.1 categorizes MLA citation elements according to the question that they answer for the three most commonly used sources: books, periodicals, and Web sites. Applying these questions to every source makes it easy to determine what information to include in a citation and how to format it. More detailed information is provided in the following chapters.

Punctuation and Formatting

The other important elements of citation writing are punctuation and formatting. These are three examples of citations to illustrate how they work.

Citation Creation Question	MLA Citation Answer
Who wrote the information used?	• Author's name
What did the author write or create?	• Title of the book or part of the book (a chapter, article, essay, short story, or poem) • Title of the periodical article • Title of the Web piece
Where is the selection found? (This question is answered only if the author's work is part of a bigger work. For example, a student might use a chapter in a book, an article in a periodical, or a page of a Web site.)	• If the writer used a part of a book, the answer to this question identifies the book. The information includes the title of the book, the name of the editor, and complete identifying information, such as edition and/or number of the volume. • For a periodical. this includes the title of the journal, magazine, or newspaper (and volume and issue for journals), date, and page numbers. • For an Internet site. this is the title of the Web site.
How was it published?	• Publication information for books includes city of publication, company, and copyright year. • Sponsor, posting date, and date of access. • All citations include source format.

Figure 2.1. Citation creation questions and MLA citation answers.

Citation for a Book

Hawking, Stephen W. *A Brief History of Time: From the Big Bang to*

    Black Holes. Toronto: Bantam, 1998. Print.

In this citation for a book, it is easy to see that three basic questions are answered: Who wrote the information used? What did the author write? and How was it published? A period follows the information that answers each question. Within the answer to the last question, the city is followed by a colon (:), and a comma separates the company from the copyright date. "Print" tells the reader that the student used a print copy of the book as opposed to a digital version. The title of the book is always in italics. The citation is double-spaced. The first line is even with the left margin, the information scans the width of the entire page, and the second line is indented ½ inch by using the hanging indent feature of paragraph formatting.

Citation for a Magazine Article

Baird, Julia. "The Savvy, Salty Political Saint." *Newsweek* 24 Dec. 2007:

    54–55. Print.

The information in a periodical citation is arranged very much like that in a book citation. The author's name is followed by a period to answer the question "Who wrote the information used?" The title of the article answers "What did the author write?" and is followed by a period. Next is the information that answers the additional question "Where is the information found?" The first piece of information that answers this question is the title of the periodical, and it is in italics, just as the title of a book would be. However, it is not enough to know that this particular article is in *Newsweek,* since it is a weekly publication. The date is also needed, so this piece of information comes next. We still have not yet completely answered the question, however, since we have not given the specific location within the cited issue. Therefore, the date is followed by a colon (most likely for the sake of clarity so that numbers will not be confused) and then the page number or numbers of the article. Finally, "Print" tells us that the researcher used the print copy of the magazine. With the question completely answered, the citation ends with a period.

Citation for a Web Page

Clark, Josh. "Does Gum Really Stay in You for Seven Years?" *How Stuff*
   Works. Discover, 18 Dec. 2007. Web. 12 Aug. 2008.

By now the citation format should begin to look familiar. It is easy
to tell that the author's name is first, followed by a period because it
answers the question "Who wrote the information used?" The title
of the article in quotation marks comes next. Usually a period would
follow the title, but there is none here because the title includes a
punctuation mark. The name of the Web site comes next to answer the
question "Where was the information found?" However, because information found on the Web can, and often does, change, it is important
to include some additional information to answer the location question.
The sponsor of the Web site helps specify the site, as well as the date of
posting. Finally, the descriptor "Web," followed by the date of access,
assures the researcher and the reader that information was available on
a specific date.

When students type their Works Cited page, they will format their
citations like these examples. In other words, each citation is double-
spaced, and there is a double space between citations. Also, MLA
citations are formatted to begin with what is called a "hanging indent."
This means that the citation begins at the margin and any additional
lines are indented one-half inch. Detailed directions for formatting
a research paper are included in Part III.

Why Not Software?

Students and teachers alike often ask if it isn't a good idea to use software to create citations. It would be so much easier to type the information into a template and let the software do the work of formatting and
punctuating. Yes, it would be so much easier to rely on software if—and
this is a big if—it could be depended upon to do the job correctly.

Here is an example of the problem, using a simple magazine citation.
The following citation is taken from the Web site NoodleBib Express:

Baird, Julia. "The Savvy, Salty Political Saint." <u>Newsweek</u> 24 Dec. 2007:
   54–55.

It is easy to see how this citation differs from the earlier example.
The software underlines this title of the magazine, which is incorrect
in the newest MLA edition, and the "Print" designation is missing.

Landmarks Son of Citation Machine at www.citationmachine.net provides the correct citation but does not use a hanging indent. The "Killer Bib Tool" at Carmun.com provides the following citation:

Baird, Julia. "The Savvy, Salty Political Saint." Newsweek Vol. 28.15

24 Dec. 2007: 54–55.

It is incorrect because it underlines the magazine title and because it includes the volume and issue numbers. Again, the "Print" designation is missing, as well.

Microsoft Office 2007 includes templates for making citations. They, too, cannot provide correct citations for all sources. For example, if the template were used to create the citation for the article from *HowStuffWorks,* it would look like this:

Clark, Josh. How Stuff Works. 18 Dec. 2007 <http://health.howstuffworks.

com/gum-seven-years.html>.

There is no place on the template to add the title of the article that was used from the Web site. Since Josh Clark may have written numerous articles for the Web site, it could be very difficult for a reader to find the correct one without the title. Since MLA no longer requires URLs to be included in citations, the citation is outdated as well as incorrect.

Software simply is not sufficiently sophisticated to formulate correct MLA citations for all contingencies. Citing this as a reason that MLA has not developed its own software, the association goes on to say: "Automated templates lack the power to provide this level of precision in documentation, and thus software programs that generate entries are not likely to be useful" (Modern Language Association).

Finally, even if software were producing correct citations, students would still have to know where to find the information in their source and type it into the correct spaces on the template. If they know how to do that and are satisfied that the resulting citation is correct, then they already know enough to create their own citations. With the help of their teachers, the media specialist, and this handbook, they will find that learning to create correct citations is not hard to do.

CHAPTER THREE

Citations for Books

Citations for books are some of the easiest citations to create. First the writer has to be able to find two important pages that are almost always located at the front of the book. The first is the title page (Figure 3.1). The title page contains most of the necessary information for the citation, including the title of the book, the person or persons responsible for the book, and the publisher. Sometimes the title page includes additional information, such as the name of the series the book is a part of or the number of the book's edition. Normally, almost all of the information found on the title page belongs in the book's citation (Figure 3.2).

The second page needed to create a citation is the copyright page (Figure 3.3). It is almost always on the back of the title page, although sometimes copyright information is on the page facing the title page. If copyright information is not in either of these two locations, then it is a good idea to check the very back of the book because a few publishers, such as DK, like to put it there.

The Difference between an Author and an Editor

Once the student has located the title page, he can now determine if he is using a book by an author or if the book has an editor. If a book is written by an author, her name will be on the title page with no identifying information. In other words, the student will never see Jane Smith, Author. If a book has an editor, her name will also appear on the title page, but she will be identified as the editor. Her name will be followed by the title "Editor," or the name might be preceded by "Edited by." If the person is not identified as an editor, then it is understood that the name is that of the author of the book (Figure 3.4).

FRONT PAGES OF A TYPICAL BOOK

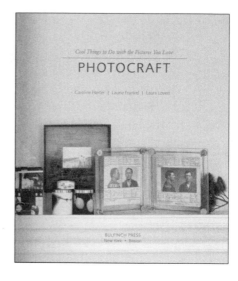

Figure 3.1. How to identify the title page of a book. From: *PHOTOCRAFT: Cool Things to Do with the Pictures You Love,* by Laurie Frankel, published by Little, Brown, & Company, used with permission.

A SAMPLE TITLE PAGE AND CITATION

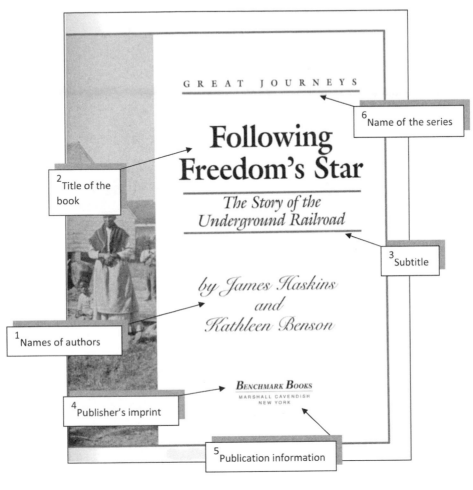

GREAT JOURNEYS

Following Freedom's Star

The Story of the Underground Railroad

by James Haskins and Kathleen Benson

BENCHMARK BOOKS
MARSHALL CAVENDISH
NEW YORK

6 Name of the series

2 Title of the book

3 Subtitle

1 Names of authors

4 Publisher's imprint

5 Publication information

     1   2   3

Haskins, James, and Kathleen Benson. *Following Freedom's Star: The Story of the*
                             4   5

   Underground Railroad. New York: Benchmark-Marshall Cavendish, 2002. Print.
     6

Great Journeys.

Figure 3.2. A sample title page and the citation for the book. The only information that might not be included in the citation is the title of the series. If it is included, it belongs at the end of the citation. Reprinted with permission from Marshall Cavendish.

A TYPICAL COPYRIGHT PAGE

Copyright © 2005 by Herter Studio LLC
Photographs copyright © 2005 by Laurie Frankel
Illustrations copyright © 2005 by Laura Lovett

All rights reserved. No part of this book may be reproduced in
any form or by any electronic or mechanical means, including
information storage and retrieval systems, without permission in
writing from the publisher, except by a reviewer who may quote
brief passages in a review.

BULFINCH PRESS

Time Warner Book Group
1271 Avenue of the Americas, New York, NY 10020
Visit our Web site at www.bulfinchpress.com

First Edition: September 2005

ISBN 0-8212-5785-4 (Scholastic Edition)
Library of Congress Control Number 2005924278

Published by arrangement with
HERTER STUDIO LLC
432 Elizabeth Street
San Francisco, CA 94114

Designed by Laura Lovett

Printed in Singapore

> Look for the copyright page on the back of the title page. The copyright date is what is needed for the citation.

Figure 3.3. A typical copyright page. From: *PHOTOCRAFT: Cool Things to Do with the Pictures You Love,* by Laurie Frankel, published by Little, Brown, & Company, used with permission.

A Book with an Author and a Book with an Editor

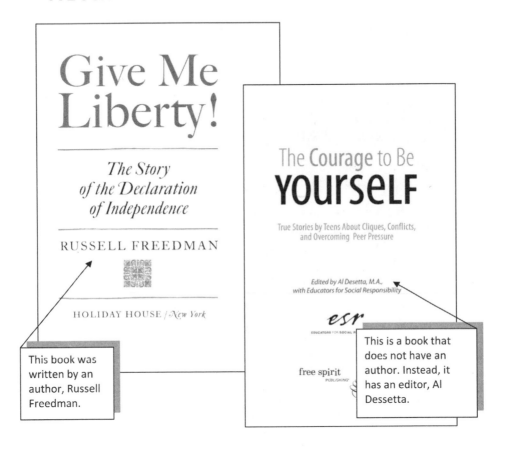

Figure 3.4. A book with an author and a book with an editor. From *Give Me Liberty! The Story of the Declaration of Independence,* published by Holiday House, reprinted with permission, and *The Courage to Be Yourself: True Stories by Teens about Cliques, Conflicts, and Overcoming Peer Pressure* by Al Desetta, ed., © 2005. Used with permission of Free Spirit Publishing, Inc., Minneapolis, MN; 800-735-7323; www.freespirit. com. All rights reserved.

Sometimes students do not know the difference between an author and an editor and why it is important to distinguish one from the other. An author, of course, is the person responsible for writing the material in the book. The words, concepts, ideas, opinions, and conclusions are her original work.

An editor, on the other hand, may be the person who has the original concept or idea for the book, but she is not the person who has actually written the entire book. Sometimes an editor may contribute the introduction, a chapter, or other piece to the book, but she will never have written the entire volume. An editor assigns or requests other authors to write portions of the book and then crafts the book by working with the participating authors. She is responsible for considerations such as the organization of the book, its length, illustrations, and layout, but in no way is she considered the writer of the book. If the book has an editor, it consists of material written by one or more authors other than the editor.

A Citation for a Book by an Author

Creating a citation for a book by an author is as easy as answering three citation creation questions: Who wrote the information used? What did the author write? and How was it published (Figure 3.5)? By looking at the title page and the copyright page of a book by an author, the student finds the answers to each of these questions.

Who Wrote the Information Used?

Students need look no further than the title page to find the author of the book. This first part of the citation is usually just one person, but

Citation Creation Question	MLA Citation Answer
Who wrote the information used?	• Author's name
What did the author write?	• Title of the book
Where is the piece found?	
How was it published?	• Publication information, meaning city of publication, company, and copyright year
	• The designation "Print"

Figure 3.5. Citation creation questions for a book by an author.

there can be two, three, or more authors. Each element on the title page is clearly labeled and accompanied by helpful explanatory information. Below the title page is the citation for that book, which can be used as a template, or model, for the student's own citations. The figures in Appendix A illustrate how to cite books by one or more than one author:

Figure A.1. A citation for a book by one author

Figure A.2. A citation for a book by more than one author

Figure A.3. A citation for a book by an author "with" others

Figure A.4. A citation for a book by an unidentified author

Figure A.5. A citation for a book by an author with a title

What Did the Author Write?

After the student cites the author, the next step in creating the citation is to answer the question "What did the author write?" The answer is the title of the book. The next figures in Appendix A are examples of how various titles are cited:

Figure A.6. A citation for a book with a subtitle

Figure A.7. A citation for a book that is an edition

Figure A.8. A citation for a graphic narrative

How Was It Published?

After the student has cited the author and title, the third and final piece of information needed for the citation answers the question "How was it published?" The answer to this question always includes three distinct bits of information: the city where the book is published, the publisher, and the copyright date. Together, these three items are called the publication information, and they always appear together in the citation. The first two bits are usually on the title page, and the third and final bit of information is on the copyright page. Following the copyright information is the fourth and final piece of information that answers the question: the designation "Print." The following figures in Appendix A are some common examples of publication information found on title pages and how they should be incorporated into citations:

Figure A.9. A citation for a book with more than one city of publication

Figure A.10. A citation for a book with a publisher's imprint

Figure A.11. A citation for a book with more than one copyright date

A Citation for a Book with an Editor

Very often, books with an editor or editors are authored by more than one person. Sometimes each author contributes a chapter or an article about a specific topic. Anthologies and similar collections may contain poems, short stories, or essays by a variety of authors. At times, the editor may also contribute to the collection, but not necessarily. In some instances, edited books may contain the work of just one author with commentary or criticism added by the editor.

When a student researcher uses an edited book, he must ask himself the same questions that apply to a book by an author: "Who wrote the information used?," "What did the author write?," and "How was it published?" Because the student is using only a specific chapter, story, or poem in the book, an additional question must also be answered. The student must answer the question "Where is the piece found?" (Figure 3.6).

Here is an example that illustrates why the additional question is necessary. Suppose a student refers to the poem "The Road Not Taken" by Robert Frost. The answer to the first question, "Who wrote the information used?," is the author, Robert Frost. The answer to the second question, "What did the author write?," is the title of the poem, "The Road Not Taken." However, that is not enough information to tell the reader where the student found the poem. That particular poem must

Citation Creation Question	MLA Citation Answer
Who wrote the information used?	• Author's name
What did the author write?	• Title of the article, chapter, essay, poem
Where is the piece found?	• Title of the book
	• Name of the editor
	• Edition used, if applicable
	• Volume number, if any
How was it published?	• City: Publisher, copyright date
	• The designation "Print"

Figure 3.6. Citation creation questions for a book with an editor.

be included in dozens, if not hundreds, of anthologies. In order for the reader to be able to find the poem in the same book that the student used, the student must answer the question "Where is the piece found?" The answer to that question is the title of the book, the name of the book's editor, and any other identifying information, such as edition or title of the multivolume set. The following examples make it easy to answer the citation creation questions correctly.

Who Wrote the Information Used?

When using an edited book, it is important for the student to pay attention to what information he is using—that of the editor or that of an author. Sometimes, as with authored books, it is appropriate to cite the entire book. At other times, it is necessary to cite the work of one or more authors within the book.

The following figures in Appendix A illustrate these three scenarios:

Figure A.12. A citation for a book with an editor

Figure A.13. A citation for a selection in an edited book

Figure A.14. A citation for two or more selections in an edited book (cross-references)

What Did the Author Write?

The answer to this question is the name of the article, essay, chapter, story, or poem that the student is citing. The title is always enclosed in quotation marks in the citation, just as it would be when referring to it in the body of the student's paper. The period that follows the title is included inside the quotation marks.

Where Is the Piece Found?

Answering this question is absolutely necessary for an edited book, as explained earlier. At this point, the student turns to the title page of the book and proceeds to add the information found there to the citation, much as he did for a book by an author. At the very least, the book's title and the name of the editor are required. If the title page has additional information, such as edition number, then that information must be included to fully identify the book.

How Was It Published?

This question is answered the same way it is for an authored book. The city of publication comes first, followed by the name of the publisher and the copyright date. The last piece of information is the designation "Print."

Citations for Multivolume Reference Sets

If the book came off the reference shelf, more information may be needed to completely identify the book. The book might be part of a multivolume set. Many reference books are multivolume. If the book is part of a multivolume set, then it usually has a number or additional title that identifies each volume of the set. It is necessary to include this additional information to identify the book as part of a set.

These figures illustrate how to correctly answer the question "Where is the piece found?" in an MLA citation:

Figure A.15. A citation for an unsigned selection in a multivolume set

Figure A.16. A citation for a signed selection in a multivolume set

Figure A.17. A citation for a titled volume in a multivolume set

Exceptions to the Rule: Encyclopedias and Dictionaries

Although the citations for most reference books are lengthier than those for authored books, the exceptions are general encyclopedias and dictionaries. These commonly used sources are easily recognizable by most writers and readers, so the citation requirements are fewer. For an encyclopedia, all that is needed is the author's name, if given, the title of the article, the name of the encyclopedia, and the edition used. For a dictionary, the entry, the book's editor, the name of the dictionary, and publication information suffice. It is important to remember, though, that specialized encyclopedias and dictionaries still require the lengthier citations of authored or edited books. These figures are examples of the correct style:

Figure A.18. A citation for a signed encyclopedia article

Figure A.19. A citation for an unsigned encyclopedia article

Figure A.20. A citation for a dictionary entry

CHAPTER FOUR

Citations for Articles in Magazines, Journals, and Newspapers

Once students know how to cite selections from an edited book, they should have no trouble citing articles from magazines, journals, and newspapers. The concept is the same: The author's specific work is part of a larger publication, both of which must be included in the citation so that readers can find the information themselves.

The concept is the same, but the citations are different in three important ways (Figure 4.1): No editor is included in a periodical citation. A periodical does not have a title page as a book does, so the name of the editor does not help to identify the publication. Also, to specify where an article is found, it is essential to include the complete date of publication for magazines and newspapers (or volume and issue information for journals) and page numbers. Periodicals are much more time-sensitive than books, so it makes sense that the date (or volume and issue) is needed to identify the publication. Just knowing an article appeared in *Sports Illustrated,* for example, does little good if the date of the publication is not provided.

The date of publication, volume, and issue number (if they are needed) can usually be found on the cover, on the spine of the magazine or journal, or on the contents page. The masthead of a newspaper includes

Citation Creation Question	MLA Citation Answer
Who wrote the information used?	• Author's name
What did the author write?	• Title of the article
Where is the piece found?	• Title of the magazine, newspaper, or journal
	• Volume and issue (journals only)
	• Date of publication
	• Page numbers
How was it published?	• The designation "Print"

Figure 4.1. Citation creation questions for an article in a periodical.

edition information, and section identifiers are usually clearly displayed with page numbers.

Having few citation elements makes citations for periodicals easy. Students will quickly learn how to create these citations.

Magazines

A magazine is a popular periodical like those commonly found for sale in places like convenience stores, drug stores, and discount stores. *Newsweek, Time, Sports Illustrated, Rolling Stone, Popular Science,* and *National Geographic* are all well-known magazines. They usually contain several articles and deal with a range of topics. Magazines are typically published weekly, monthly, or bimonthly.

A citation for an article in a magazine is included in Appendix B:

Figure B.1. A citation for an article in a magazine

Journals

Journals are different from magazines. Usually, journals are written for an academic or professional readership. Their focus is narrow, and their articles are often peer reviewed. This means that, instead of having a large writing staff employed by the publication, readers submit articles that are reviewed by a panel of professional peers who advise the editorial staff. Journals are often published by professional organizations or by colleges and universities.

The major difference between a journal and a magazine in terms of citation elements is the inclusion of volume and issue information. When citing a magazine, volume and issue information are not included, even if they are printed in the magazine. A journal citation, on the other hand, does include volume and issue information. A sample citation is shown in Appendix B:

Figure B.2. A citation for an article in a journal

Newspapers

Newspapers are usually daily or weekly periodicals written to appeal to a wide variety of readers in a specific city, town, or region. They cover topics of general interest, such as national, state, and local news, sports, business, and entertainment. In citing articles in newspapers, students must take into account some unique considerations. One is that the place of publication is often included in the title of the newspaper. If it is not, then it is important to put it in the citation. Otherwise, the reader would not know which city's publication of *The State* or *The Chronicle,* for example, the writer was referring to.

Another element that makes newspapers unique is that there can be more than one edition of a day's publication. For example, there may be an early-morning and a late edition that include different information and different pagination. Including the edition, if given, is important when citing newspaper articles. Finally, pages in newspapers are often numbered differently from pages in other periodicals since newspapers have sections. Including the section is important when citing a newspaper article. Figure B.3 is a sample of a correct citation.

Figure B.3. A citation for a newspaper article

CHAPTER FIVE

Citing Information from Online Sources

Teachers and media specialists cringe when a student asks for help citing an online source. From e-mail to wikis and everything in between, online sources can be problematic. For one thing, there is no guarantee that the same information that is there today will be there tomorrow. Maybe the entire source will be gone! Maybe the source will still be there, but how reliable is its information?

Ideally, students should have several guided experiences in selecting and evaluating Web sites before they use the Web for research. They should know what different URL extensions, such as .com, .gov, and .edu, mean and what kinds of information they can expect at these and other sites. They should be able to recognize the difference between fact and opinion. They should question an author's credentials since it is possible for anyone to post on the Web. They should know to look for currency and accuracy and to be wary of sites with outdated or inaccurate information and broken links.

For students who have not had sufficient practice in Web site selection, one no-cost alternative to letting them "Google" is for the teacher and the media specialist to create a digital folder of preselected Web sites and place it on computer desk tops or an accessible drive for students to use. With this strategy, the students will know that they are accessing credible information, and the educators can be assured that students will be successful in their search for reliable information.

Another possibility is the purchase of an Internet program that links Web sites to the online catalog. Major circulation software companies supply this feature, and there are other products available, as well.

An additional strategy is to use Internet databases. Several vendors have various products that make student searches easy, productive, fast, and accurate. Whether students are directed to preselected Web sites or to digital databases, students and teachers alike can be assured that they are accessing quality sources.

Citing Online Sources

One of the traditional challenges for teachers and media specialists when teaching online citations has been to teach their students to distinguish among the variety of resources available via computer. Not only did students have to learn to evaluate sites' credibility, accuracy, and currency, but also they had to learn to distinguish one type of source from another so that they cited each source correctly. Now, with the seventh edition of the *MLA Handbook,* citations for Web sources are easier to craft.

Students need to know how to recognize just three types of sources that they find on the Internet. The first category is very broad and includes nearly everything they find on the Web. The second category is scholarly journals, and the third includes articles found in online databases.

That said, the *MLA Handbook* allows the flexibility for researchers to add more information to citations if they choose to do so. For example, if the information on the Web appeared in another format first, then the student may begin the citation with the information for the original source and end the citation with the Web information. Including original source citation information is optional for all Web citations except articles found in databases.

Although the reader may benefit by knowing that the information the student used was originally available in another format, such information adds little, if any, value to a research assignment. A citation formatted in this way also seems to put more emphasis on the original source than on the location where the student found the information. In addition, such citations are longer and therefore harder for students to create. For these reasons, it is recommended that students learn how to format the information for the source where they find it (the Web) and omit the extraneous material, except for information from online databases.

Another big difference in the newest edition of the *MLA Handbook* is that the requirement for URLs at the end of citations has been dropped. Because Web addresses change frequently and because the same material may be found at more than one Web site, the Modern Language Association has omitted URLs as a required citation element. They may, however, be added by the teacher or the student if citation elements do not make it clear where the student found the information. For the sake of simplicity, URLs are not included herein.

Students can create citations for almost anything they find on the Web by answering a few citation creation questions (Figure 5.1). The figures in Appendix C illustrate citations for nearly every Web source.

Information on the Web

The illustrations in Figures C.1 through C.7 are for information found on the Web. Although they represent a wide variety of sources and material, the citations are all formatted the same way. Students will learn to craft these citations quickly. The following figures show the correct style for various online citations:

Figure C.1. A citation for an article in an online encyclopedia

Figure C.2. A citation for a Web page

Figure C.3. A citation for a Web site

Figure C.4. A citation for an article on a wiki

Figure C.5. A citation for a blog or discussion board entry

Citation Creation Question	MLA Citation Answer
Who wrote the information used?	• Author's name, if given
What did the author write?	• Title of the e-mail, blog, Web page, etc.
Where is the piece found?	• Title of the Web site
How was it published?	• Sponsor, if any
	• Date of posting or update
	• The designation "Web"
	• Date of access

Figure 5.1. Citation creation questions for online sources.

Figure C.6. A citation for an article in an online periodical

Figure C.7. A citation for nonprint material on the Web

A Scholarly Journal

A citation for an online scholarly journal is formatted much like a citation for an online periodical.

Figure C.8. A citation for an article in an online scholarly journal

Information on the Web in an Online Database

Citations for sources included in an online database need more information than other Internet sources. Because the information was published before it appeared online, the publication information is included in the citation as well.

Figure C.9. A citation for an article in an online database

E-mail

If a student has corresponded with someone who is considered an authority or if she has conducted an interview by e-mail, then it can be used as a credible source. A sample citation is shown in Figure C.10:

Figure C.10. A citation for an e-mail

Note: Citations for materials in online databases that also appear in print are lengthier. Complete instructions for these citations appear in Appendix C, Figure C.9.

CHAPTER SIX

Citations for Miscellaneous Sources

Information, it seems, is everywhere, and it is always possible to find valuable facts, statistics, ideas, and opinions in places other than books, periodicals, and the Internet. Sources such as television and radio programs, films, performances, artwork, speeches, and interviews all have the potential for providing up-to-the-minute data as well as fresh perspectives on virtually any topic.

Miscellaneous sources generally include media other than those that are in print or computer accessed. Live performances of plays, operas, symphonies, and rock concerts can be cited. So can television and radio programs, films, recorded music, music videos, and live interviews. Sculpture and cartoons can also be included as cited sources.

Citations for miscellaneous sources are similar in some ways to all other citations. Most begin with the person responsible for the work, then list the work and other pertinent information. There are differences, however. First, because of the characteristics of miscellaneous sources, the information included in them is often unique. No other type of citation, for example, might list performers or the call letters of a broadcasting station. Second, it is almost always necessary to include in the citation a description of the medium cited, such as videocassette or personal interview.

Additionally, it is sometimes important to determine whether to begin a citation with the name of an individual or the title of the production or performance. An example helps to illustrate: Usually, a citation for a film, television, or radio program begins with the title of the work. If, however, a student were analyzing the work of a particular director, he would begin the citations for the director's films with the name of the director.

As media specialists, teachers, and student researchers craft citations for miscellaneous sources, they should keep in mind that one of the criteria for judging whether a citation is well written is whether it leads the readers to the same information that the writer used. To do that, the citation should contain the correct elements, and they should also be formatted to emphasize the elements that are the most important to the researcher's work.

Because of the unique nature of miscellaneous sources, it helps to modify the wording of the citation creation questions slightly in order for them to be pertinent to the material being cited. Figure 6.1 illustrates how better to ask the questions so that the correct information is included in citations. Teachers and students should also keep in mind that the order of the first two citation creation questions may be switched in order to make a more relevant citation.

Citation Creation Question	MLA Citation Answer
Who created the piece used?*	• Name of artist, performer, director, or other pertinent person
What is the title of the piece?	• Title of the artwork, music, movie, etc.
Where is the piece found?	• This information varies, depending upon what is being cited. See the examples in Appendix D.
How was it published?	• Recording label, film distributor, broadcasting station, or other means of distribution, and date. See examples in Appendix D.
	• The format of the source

Figure 6.1. Citation creation questions for a miscellaneous source.

The following figures in Appendix D exemplify the types of citations that students may need to create for miscellaneous sources:

Figure D.1. Citations for recorded music

Figure D.2. Citations for film

Figure D.3. Citations for works of art

Figure D.4. Citations for television and radio programs

Figure D.5. Citations for live performances, speeches, and lectures

Figure D.6. Citations for interviews

PART TWO

Parenthetical Documentation

CHAPTER SEVEN

Summarizing, Paraphrasing, and Quoting

As discussed in previous chapters, plagiarism is a mistake that teachers and media specialists want to help students avoid. It is not enough to tell students that copying is wrong. Students need to see examples of plagiarism so that they can understand what is acceptable and what is not.

When a student finds material that he wants to use in his research, he has four choices: He can summarize, paraphrase, quote, or plagiarize. Often, he does the last, albeit unintentionally. Students need to know that it is not enough to change a few words in a sentence or change the sentence structure using the same words; they are still plagiarizing. They need to know what works and what does not when it comes to using other people's words.

For example, here is a quotation from Theodore R. Sizer's book *The Red Pencil:*

What makes public education special in America's democracy is the absolute requirement that citizens of a certain age attend schools and that governments raise the moneys to pay for those schools (35).

In attempting to use the idea without quoting the sentence, a student might try to substitute synonyms and change the sentence slightly, something like this:

What makes public schools special in America is the obligation for children to go to school until they reach a certain age and that the government will pay for it.

Changing the sentence in this way may satisfy the student that he is in the clear, but he would be wrong. To use that sentence without documenting the idea as Sizer's would be plagiarism. Simply substituting a few synonymous words and phrases does not make the idea original to the student. The challenge for students is to learn to express someone else's ideas in their own words and style. Then they need to remember to cite their source.

Summarizing

Being able to write good summaries is one of the essential tools of good researchers. Not only does this ability help the student avoid plagiarism, but also it helps to ensure that the student truly understands the material he has read. To summarize, a student must read a passage of material—it could be a paragraph or an entire section—devoted to one concept and then state the idea succinctly in his own words. He should state the idea in a way that makes sense to him.

Summaries should be brief. A sentence or two for every concept should suffice. If a student is taking notes, he should label his cards with "summary" or with an "S" so that he remembers that the words are his own. He will still need to acknowledge the source of the information or idea in his writing, since the idea is not his own. This is done with parenthetical documentation, discussed in Chapter Eight, and with a citation on the Works Cited page.

Paraphrasing

If a summary does not suffice for capturing the ideas of an author, a student may decide to use a paraphrase. By paraphrasing, the student uses his own words and sentence structure, but he expresses more detail than he would with a summary. Paraphrasing is useful if the student does not want to quote the author's words exactly but wants to convey more than the essence of his idea. For example, a student might paraphrase Sizer's sentence this way:

Free mandatory schooling for every child in this country is a charac-
teristic that makes our educational system distinctive.

This sentence captures the essence of Sizer's thought without using his words or sentence structure. Again, the student should label his notes as a "paraphrase" or "P" so that he will be assured later at the writing stage that the words are his own. The idea is still Sizer's, however, and so a citation and parenthetical documentation are required.

Quoting

Sometimes it is appropriate to use direct quotes when writing a research paper. Perhaps a writer has expressed himself in a distinctive way that captures what the student wants to express. Perhaps facts and figures are pertinent to a student's thesis. If a student is analyzing literature, then it is appropriate for his paper to include several quoted passages from the selection.

Normally, however, quotations are used sparingly. Students should not get into the habit of using long, extensive quotations if the material could have been summarized or paraphrased. Quotations are reserved for those times when the writer's own words are essential to what the student wants to say.

Using the example from Sizer, a student might incorporate a quotation in this way:

Sizer maintains that free mandatory schooling for every "citizen
of a certain age" in this country is a characteristic that makes our
educational system distinctive.

By writing the sentence in this way, the student has paraphrased Sizer's idea by putting it in his own words. He has also included a short quotation of a distinctive phrase that he thinks is important. By crafting this sentence, the student has avoided plagiarism. He has used his own words and sentence structure. The words that he took from Sizer's text are enclosed in quotation marks, and they are quoted exactly. The only things needed to make it complete are parenthetical documentation and a citation on the Works Cited page.

When a student uses quotations, he must be very careful to copy the word, phrase, or passage exactly as it is written, even if it includes misspellings or incorrect grammar or punctuation. When taking notes he should make sure to label it as a "quotation" or with a "Q," and he should take care to put quotation marks where they belong, especially if he has also summarized or paraphrased in the notation.

What Teachers and Media Specialists Can Do

Teachers and media specialists can help students learn to summarize, paraphrase, and quote well in advance of undertaking research assignments. Once students know how to identify key words and main ideas, they can learn to summarize and paraphrase. Completing mini-lessons and practice sessions before beginning a research assignment help give students the abilities and confidence they will need when the research assignment arrives.

A good way to practice before undertaking the research project is to make the practice sessions part of the research. In the weeks preceding the research assignment, students can practice summarizing, paraphrasing, and quoting sources that they will be using for research. This way, they will already have some of their notes made when the assignment begins, and they will have the skills to proceed without the anxiety and frustration of starting from scratch.

It is more than important to make sure that students are in command of these skills—it is essential. If teachers and media specialists do not take care to arm students with the proficiencies they need to be good researchers, then they will have no one but themselves to blame when students plagiarize. Equipped with the right tools and involved in engaging research, most students will make the right choices.

CHAPTER EIGHT

Parenthetical Documentation

Knowing how to craft citations for all of the many sources that students might use in their research is important, but it is only half of the process. The other half is the ability to incorporate the source information into the texts of their papers or other final products. Imbedding sources within text is called parenthetical documentation. Using parenthetical documentation allows the student to indicate exactly where the cited facts, ideas, opinions, and quotations are found in any given source.

Much like other aspects of research and writing, incorporating parenthetical documentation accurately and well is a skill that involves repeated practice. Students need to be aware of two essential criteria for good parenthetical documentation: accuracy and readability. Accuracy simply means that the reader will find the cited information in the source where the writer has indicated. Readability points to the student's ability to incorporate parenthetical documentation without distracting the reader from the flow of the text.

Accuracy

In most cases, sending a reader to a specific page in a source simply means indicating the last name of the author and the page number where the information is found. For example, if a student used some information from page 15 of this book, he would indicate that in his text by including parenthetical documentation that looks like this: (Heath 15). The last name of the author directs the reader to the Works

Cited page, where he will find the citation for this book. He can then obtain a copy, turn to page 15, and find exactly what the student found.

The information contained in a parenthetical documentation depends upon the citation it is based upon. The purpose of parenthetical documentation is to direct the reader to the appropriate citation, so it must contain enough information to do that without becoming unwieldy and distracting the reader from the flow of the paper. Questions and problems can arise. What if the Works Cited page contains two books authored by Heath? What if there are two or more authors for a book? What about an article from the Web that has no page numbers?

These and other issues can and do surface when students incorporate research findings into their own writing. The good news is that there are solutions for all parenthetical documentation problems. Most solutions are listed in Figure 8.1. If the answer to a student's dilemma is not found there, the answer can be determined by using a common-sense approach. Solve the problem by asking the question: What information will point the reader to the source used? The answer is always the first piece of information in the citation. Shorten it, if necessary, but never to the point that it cannot be clearly identified. Include page numbers, if applicable.

Readability

While accuracy is crucial, readability is highly desirable. If one has to be sacrificed in order to achieve the other, readability should always fall by the wayside. That does not mean, however, that students should be allowed to be sloppy or careless with their parenthetical documentation. Readability is what keeps the reader turning the pages. It is a substantial part of what makes a paper or project successful. It is a reflection of good writing skills, which, like everything else connected to research, need to be practiced often and in a variety of ways.

Readability in conjunction with parenthetical documentation means that the documentation intrudes as little as possible upon the text. Because the writer wants the reader to focus on the points he is making, parenthetical documentation is best kept as brief as possible. The writer must also decide when parenthetical documentation is needed in the text. A "more is better" approach is not necessarily a good one if the documentation constantly interferes with readability and makes it appear that the writer contributed no critical thinking of his own.

PARENTHETICAL DOCUMENTATION FOR ACCURACY

A work by a single author. It does not matter what the person created—a book, an article, a painting. The last name followed by appropriate page number (if there is one) is all that is needed. Place the information inside parentheses before the period of the sentence.

Examples: The most recent animal added to the endangered species list is the polar bear (Jenkins 12).

A work by two or three authors. Use the last names of the authors and the page number or numbers.

Example: Painting a room is one of the least expensive ways to redecorate (Colson and Mills 31).

Example: Music experts agree that blues originated in the United States (Harner, Sturgill, and Durham 45).

A work by four or more authors. Use the last name of the first author and et al. and the page numbers.

Example: Electromagnetic waves of varying lengths and properties make up the electromagnetic spectrum (Peters et al. 139–45).

Two or more works by one author. Use the last name and the full or shortened version of the appropriate title with the page number or numbers. A comma follows the author's name.

Example: Hawaii was the last state to be admitted to the union (Baker, *Facts about the 50 States* 47).

It would be appropriate to shorten the title to *Facts*. It would not be permissible to shorten it to *States* because the reader needs to see the first word of the title in the parenthetical documentation so that the citation is easy to find.

Two authors with the same last name. If the Works Cited page has two or more authors with the same last name, add the first initial in the parenthetical documentation.

Example: Nearly 32% of teachers nationwide have a graduate degree (L. Anderson 15).

Figure 8.1. Parenthetical documentation for accuracy. *(Continued)*

A work listed by title. Use the title of the work or a shortened form if it is long and page numbers, if any.

Example: During World War II the Japanese experimented with ways to drop bombs from hydrogen-filled balloons ("Japanese").

Works Cited

"Japanese Balloon Bomb." *History Detectives*. PBS. WNTV, Greenville. 13 July
    2008. Television.

An entire work or one with no page numbers. When citing an entire work, it is standard practice to use the author or title (whatever is the first element of the citation) in the text. Then no parenthetical documentation is necessary. (See Figure 8.2.)

Figure 8.1. *(Continued)*

To enhance readability, the writer also wants to place parenthetical documentation as near as possible to the information cited, but at natural breaks in the text. In most instances, the best place is before the period that ends a sentence. It is not the only place, however, since there are various methods to incorporate parenthetical documentation without sacrificing readability. Many are illustrated in Figure 8.2. Students who have the opportunity to practice frequently will improve both the accuracy and readability of their parenthetical documentation.

PARENTHETICAL DOCUMENTATION FOR READABILITY

Summarizing or paraphrasing part of a work. When citing part of a work, the writer has two ways to integrate the parenthetical documentation. She can use the method exemplified in Figure 8.1, in which the author's name and the page number both appear in the parenthetical documentation. Or she can incorporate the author's name into the text of the paper and include only the page number in the parenthetical documentation.

Examples: The most recent animal added to the endangered species list is the polar bear (Jenkins 12).

Jenkins reports that the most recent animal added to the endangered species list is the polar bear (12).

Painting a room is one of the least expensive ways to redecorate (Colson and Mills 31).

According to Colson and Mills, painting a room is one of the least expensive ways to redecorate (31).

Summarizing an entire work. When referring to an entire work, whether it is a book, Web site, interview, or television program, it is best to include the reference in the text of the paper with no parenthetical documentation. The text must include the first item in the citation, whether it is a person or a title.

Example: John McCain outlined his plan for Iraq during his recent appearance on *Meet the Press.*

Works Cited

McCain, John. Interview. Tim Russert. *Meet the Press.* NBC. WABC, Charleston. 12 Feb. 2008. Television.

Quoting from a work. Quotations can be included in texts in two ways. Brief quotations are incorporated into the narrative of the text. When a brief quotation is used, the parenthetical documentation is placed immediately after the closing quotation mark but before the period. The author may or may not be integrated into the text.

Example: Sizer maintains that mandatory education should be defined "in terms of performance rather than school attendance" (25).

Figure 8.2. Parenthetical documentation for readability. *(Continued)*

Mandatory education would improve if it were defined "in terms of performance rather than school attendance" (Sizer 25).

Quotations that are longer than four lines should be set off from the text. Usually the sentence before the quote ends with a colon. The quoted text is indented one inch from the left margin and double spaced. Do not use any quotation marks.

Example: In his essay "The Truth about the World," Lloyd Alexander summarizes what he learned about life from his first date that never happened:

> The incident taught me the truth about the world. It is not a good place. Life is ruled by unfair and malicious fate, filled with injustice, humiliation, shame, despair, tears and woe, misery undiluted. Naturally I became a writer. I didn't know how to dance anyway. (14).

Poetry can be quoted by including up to three lines within the text of the paper.

Example: Emily Dickinson, known for creating vivid images with few words, writes, "There is no frigate like a book / To take us lands away" (32).

If more than three lines of poetry are quoted, they should be set off from the body of the paper by indenting one inch, just as with a long quotation of prose. Do not use quotation marks.

Example: Emily Dickinson is known for creating vivid images with few words:

> There is no frigate like a book
>
> To take us lands away,
>
> Nor any coursers like a page
>
> Of prancing poetry. (32)

Figure 8.2. *(Continued)*

PART THREE

Formatting

CHAPTER NINE

The Works Cited Page

The Works Cited page should be the next page after the conclusion of the paper and should include all the sources that are cited in the body of the paper but no more. If a source was consulted but not used to document the paper, then it should not be included on the Works Cited page. Only sources that were used for parenthetical documentation should be listed.

- Start the Works Cited page on a new page. It should follow the last page of the text and should be numbered consecutively. For example, if the last page of the text is 5, then the Works Cited page is page 6.

- The Works Cited page is double spaced. The title Works Cited (not italicized) is centered on the page one inch from the top. Double space and begin listing the works cited.

- Citations are arranged in alphabetical order by the first word of the citation. The only exception to this rule is this: If a citation begins with a title and the title begins with the words *A, An,* or *The,* use the next word to alphabetize. For example, if an unsigned article entitled "The Reasons Why Johnny Can't Read" is cited, it will be alphabetized by the word *Reasons.*

- Each citation is double spaced, and there is one double space between citations. In other words, all the lines are equally spaced, just as the body of the paper is.

- Each citation starts at the left margin and continues to the right margin, if needed. Subsequent lines are indented one-half inch. This is called a hanging indent. Format the word processing software to do this automatically. See Chapter Ten for detailed instructions.

- If citing two or more authors with the same last name, then alphabetize by their first names or initials. For example, Anderson, J. comes before Anderson, L., and Anderson, Adam is placed before Anderson, Thomas.

- If citing more than one work by a single author, alphabetize by the first word of the title of the work. Type the author's name for the first citation only. For the succeeding citations, type three hyphens and a period. Then proceed with the rest of the citation. For example:

Anderson, Lorin. "School Reform in South Carolina: Where

We Stand." *Carolina Review* June 1997: 37–42.

---. *What's Right with Our Schools.* Columbia: Prentiss, 1997.

213–279.

Because these two works have the same author, they are alphabetized by the first word of the titles, *School* and *What's.* See Figure 9.1 for an example of a Works Cited page.

There are two ways to make sure the Works Cited page is complete and correct. Both methods should be used—first one, then the other.

- Make sure the sources in all parenthetical documentations are listed in the Works Cited page.

- Make sure that every citation in the Works Cited page is used in a parenthetical documentation.

By checking both ways, the writer can be sure that every source used is included in the Works Cited and, conversely, that there are no citations in the Works Cited that do not show up in the body of the paper.

Baird, Julia. "The Savvy, Salty Political Saint." *Newsweek* 24 Dec. 2007: 54+. Print.

Copeland, Larry. "Distractions Challenge Teen Drivers." *USA Today* 25 Jan. 2007: n. pag. *SIRS Knowledge Source.* Web. 5 Oct. 2007.

Feel the Noise! Chicago: Raintree, 2006. Print.

Freedman, Russell. *Give Me Liberty! The Story of the Declaration of Independence.* New York: Holiday, 2000. Print.

Grady, Michael P., Kristine C. Helbling, and Dennis R. Lubeck. "Teacher Professionalism Since *A Nation at Risk.*" *Phi Delta Kappan* 89 (2008): 603+. Print.

The Grapes of Wrath. Dir. John Ford. Perf. Henry Fonda. Twentieth Century-Fox, 1967. Videocassette.

Herter, Caroline, Laurie Frankel, and Laura Lovett. *Photocraft: Cool Things to Do with the Pictures You Love.* New York: Bulfinch, 2005. Print.

Miller, Paul. "The Art and Skill of Biographical Writing." Museum of Education, University of South Carolina. 15 Mar. 2006. Lecture.

Schroeder, Peter W. and Dagmar Schroeder-Hildebrand. *Six Million Paper Clips: The Making of a Children's Holocaust Memorial.* Minneapolis: Kar-Ben, 2004. Print.

Shone, Rob. *Volcanoes.* New York: Rosen Central, 2007. Print.

Figure 9.1. An example of a Works Cited page.

CHAPTER TEN

Formatting a Paper in MLA Format

Once the paper is polished, it should be typed on a computer and printed. MLA has specific rules about the layout of the paper. The paper must be double spaced throughout. All margins must be set at one inch. It is a good idea to select a common font, such as Arial or New Times Roman, in 12 point. Students are often tempted to use a script or other fancy font in a large size. However, these choices are never acceptable for an MLA-formatted paper.

Students also like to add a fancy title page, often with artistic flourishes. Research papers in MLA format should not have title pages unless the teacher requires or allows one. Otherwise, the first page of the paper must look like the example in Figure 10.1.

All pages have a one-inch margin at the top, as well as one-inch margins on the sides and the bottom, just like the first page. If the paper has as Appendix, it begins on a new page after the body of the paper. The Works Cited page always comes last and begins on a page by itself. Page numbers continue throughout the paper to the end of the Works Cited page.

Formatting the Paper in Microsoft Word '97 or 2003

It is easy to use Microsoft Word to format an MLA paper. If the version of Microsoft Office is '97 or 2003, then the following procedures will ensure correct formatting.

- Open a new document in Word

- Go to File, then Page Setup to set the one-inch margins

- Go to Format, then Paragraph to set the first-line indentation of paragraphs to 0.5 inch and to set up double spacing.

- Go to View, then Header and Footer to set up the Header with page numbers and with the student's last name. Be sure that the font for the header is the same as that for the paper and that it is set at 12 point.

When the student is ready to type the Works Cited page, she will have to make the following changes so that the citations will be formatted correctly.

- Go to Insert, then Break to start a New Page for Works Cited.

- Go to Format, then Paragraph to set the Hanging Indent to type the Works Cited page.

- Make sure to keep the line spacing at double.

Each citation should be double spaced, and there should be a double space between citations. (See the sample Works Cited page in Chapter Nine.)

Formatting the Paper in Microsoft Word 2007

Microsoft Word 2007 looks and acts much different from earlier versions of the software. If the user has not already done so, it is necessary to reset some of the defaults in order to comply with MLA guidelines. For example, the Paragraph Spacing settings for Before, After, and At should all be set at 0 point because the default is not correct for MLA formatting. Be sure to change the left and right margins to one inch. The font should be set at Arial or Times New Roman 12 point instead of the default, which is 11 point Calibri.

- Go to Insert, then Header to set up the page numbers with last name and page number. Be sure to change the font to the one used for the paper. Change the size to 12 point.

- When you are ready to begin typing the Works Cited page, you will need to change the Paragraph settings under the Home tab.

- Go to Insert, then Page Break to start a new page for Works Cited.

- Go to Home, then Paragraph, then Indentation to set the hanging indent for the Works Cited page.
- Make sure the indentations are set at.5 inch.

Common Formatting Mistakes

- Do not type the paper's title in bold type or all caps.
- Do not underline the paper's title.
- Do not use the space bar to indent paragraphs or subsequent lines of citations.
- Do not type Works Cited in bold or italics or underline it.
- Do not put the final paper in a binder of any kind unless the teacher asks for one.

FORMATING AN MLA PAPER

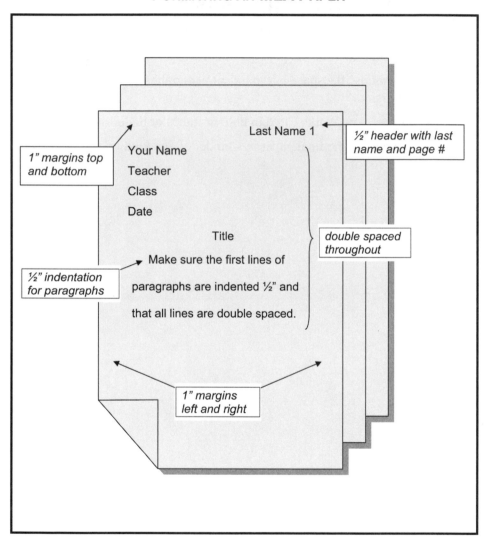

Figure 10.1. Formatting an MLA paper. It is important to follow all MLA guidelines when typing a paper in MLA format.

Citation Basics Quick Facts

What Do I Do If...?

The Author of the Material I Used...

- has a preposition before his or her last name?
    - Generally speaking, treat propositions, such as Von, Di, Da, and Del, as part of the last name. Create the citation and alphabetize as if it were the beginning of the last name.
- wrote more than one book or article that I used?
    - On the Works Cited page, alphabetize letter by letter. So Smith, John. *Remembering Dad* would come before Smith, John. *Remembering Mom.*
    - On the Works Cited page, multiple works by the same author are entered like this:

    Smith, John. *Remembering Dad.*

    ---. *Remembering Mom.*

    - The three hyphens represent the exact author or authors in the citation immediately above. If there are any differences, type out the names in full in the subsequent citation. If *Remembering Mom* had been written by John Smith and Jane Smith, the second entry would be:

    Smith, John, and Jane Smith. *Remembering Mom.*

    - In parenthetical documentation, to avoid confusion, add a short-ened version of the title, such as (Smith, *Dad* 56).
- isn't a person; it's a corporation?
    - Use the name of the corporation or government agency as the author. Be sure to write it out; do not use abbreviations. Also, do not use articles to begin the name. For example, AMA would be written as American Medical Association, not The American Medical Association.
    - Sometimes the corporate or government author is also the pub-lisher. That is okay; list the entity as both in the citation if that is what it is.

The Title of An Article or Book...

- is written in all capital letters?
  - Capitalize the first and last words plus all important words in a title, regardless of how it is written on the title page.
- ends with a punctuation mark of its own?
  - Omit the period at the end of the title in a citation.
  - If the title ends with its own punctuation and has a subtitle, omit the colon before the subtitle.
- includes a number?
  - Write the number as it is given in the title.
  - If the number is at the beginning of the title, alphabetize it according to the letter it would be if written (e.g.,101 Dalmatians would be alphabetized by the letter *O*).
- includes an ampersand (&)?
  - Write the ampersand as the word "and."
- includes another title?
  - If the title of a book or Web site includes another title (e.g., *An Analysis of* Romeo and Juliet, italicize the title of the book, but do not italicize the title within the title.
  - If the title of an article includes the title of a book or play, italicize it, as in "An Analysis of *Romeo and Juliet*."
  - If the title of an article includes the title of a poem or short story, use single quotations (apostrophes) for the enclosed title, as in "An Analysis of Emily Dickinson's 'I Heard a Fly Buzz When I Died.'"
- begins with an article—*a, an,* or *the*?
  - Normally, this is not an issue, but if the work has no author, it is alphabetized by the title. The article should be ignored but not omitted. For example, "A Day in the Life of My Cat Gracie" (no author) would by alphabetized by the letter *D* but written as shown.

Some of the Information I Need for a Citation Is Missing?

- For a book, use these abbreviations:
  - No copyright date: n.d.
  - No publisher: N.p.

- No city: N.p.
- No page numbers: n.pag.
- No author or editor: Start with the title of the book or piece used.
- For other print sources:
  - No author or editor: Start with the title of the piece used.
  - No page numbers: n.pag.
  - Other missing information: Skip it and go to the next part of the citation.
- For Web sources:
  - If there is no author or editor: Start with the title of the piece.
  - If there is no sponsor or publisher, use N.p.
  - If there is no posting date or copyright date, use n.d.
  - Always include the date of access.

Appendix A:
Examples of Citations for Books

A Citation for a Book by one Author

- This is the easiest and most basic of citations. It answers the three questions a citation must address:

  - Who wrote the information used?

  - What did he write?

  - How was it published?

- By arranging the information in proper MLA format, readers will know

  - Who was responsible for the information cited

  - Where to find it

- All other citations for books by authors, no matter how much information they contain, follow the same format, answer the same three questions, and give the reader the same information.

CITATION BASICS:

- Never change or shorten an author's name. If there is a middle name or initial, it follows the first name in the citation, followed by a period.
- Use standard rules of capitalization in citations. In other words, do not write THE LIFE AND DEATH OF ADOLF HITLER in the citation even if it appears in all caps on the title page. It should be written in upper and lower case.
- Do not use bold type or fancy fonts because a title page has been designed that way. Use standard 12 pt. type fonts.
- If an ampersand (&) appears in a title or subtitle, substitute the word "and." Otherwise, type the title as it appears, using standard rules of capitalization.
- If the title includes numbers, do not spell them out; include them as written.

A Citation for a Book by One Author

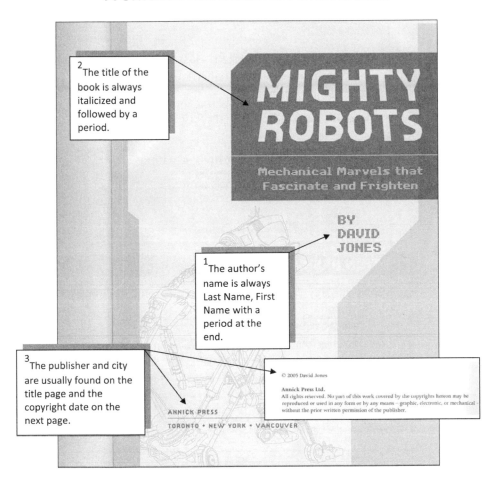

^{2}The title of the book is always italicized and followed by a period.

^{1}The author's name is always Last Name, First Name with a period at the end.

^{3}The publisher and city are usually found on the title page and the copyright date on the next page.

```
      1                        2
Jones, David. Mighty Robots: Mechanical Marvels That Fascinate and Frighten.
          3
      Toronto: Annick, 2005. Print.
```

Figure A.1. A citation for a book by one author. Mighty Robots: Mechanical Marvels that Fascinate and Frighten by David Jones, published by Annick Press (2005) used with permission.

A Citation for a Book by More Than One Author

Pay careful attention to the authors' names in this citation.

❏ Put the authors' names in the order that they are listed on the title page.

❏ The first author's name is inverted—last name, first name. This is always done for purposes of alphabetizing the Works Cited page. Do not invert any other names.

❏ The first author's middle initial (if there is one) follows the first name.

❏ All other authors' names are left in their natural order.

❏ A comma follows the first author's name.

CITATION BASICS:

- A book with three authors on the title page would be cited like this:
  - Smith, John, Bob James, and Mary Jones.
  - Notice the commas.
- If the book has four or more authors it is acceptable to substitute *et al* (Latin for *and others*) for the names after the first name.
  - Smith, John, Bob James, Mary Jones, and Jim Brown. *or*
  - Smith, John, et al.
  - Notice the commas.
- Always end a citation for a book with the designation *Print*.

A CITATION FOR A BOOK BY MORE THAN ONE AUTHOR

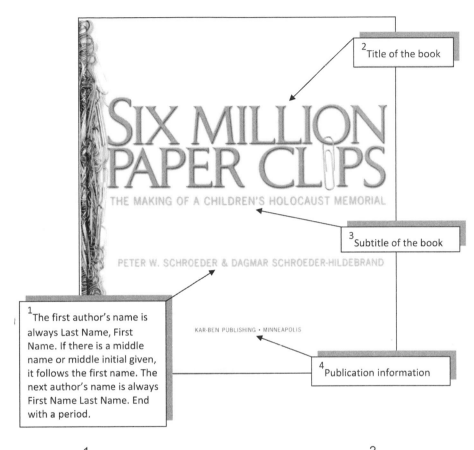

2 Title of the book

3 Subtitle of the book

1 The first author's name is always Last Name, First Name. If there is a middle name or middle initial given, it follows the first name. The next author's name is always First Name Last Name. End with a period.

4 Publication information

1   2
Schroeder, Peter W., and Dagmar Schroeder-Hildebrand. *Six Million Paper Clips: The*
3   4
Making of a Children's Holocaust Memorial. Minneapolis: Kar-Ben, 2004. Print.

Figure A.2. A citation for a book by more than one author. *Six Million Paper Clips* by Peter W. Schroeder and Dagmar Schroeder-Hildebrand. Text copyright © 2004 by Peter W. Schroeder and Dagmar Schroeder-Hildebrand. Reprinted with the permission of Kar-Ben Publishing, a division of Lerner Publishing Group, Inc. All rights reserved. No part of this text excerpt may be used or reproduced in any manner whatsoever without the prior written permission of Lerner publishing Group, Inc.

A Citation for a Book by an Author "with" Others

❑ Usually when a book has multiple authors, they appear one after another, as in the preceding example.

❑ Sometimes a principal author will be listed and another author or authors will also be designated, often below the first author's name and in smaller type. When additional authors are listed in this way the word "and" or "with" will usually precede the names.

❑ Use the word on the title page to designate additional authors (in this case the word "with" is used, so it is included in the citation).

CITATION BASICS:

• Notice that the title "Historian" and the degree "Ph.D." are not included in the citation.

A CITATION FOR A BOOK BY AN AUTHOR "WITH" OTHERS

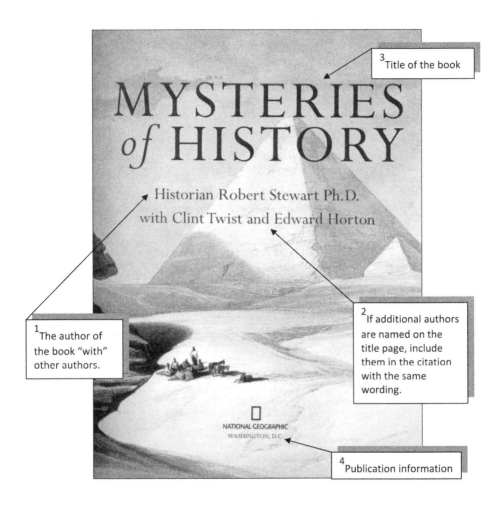

3 Title of the book

MYSTERIES *of* HISTORY

Historian Robert Stewart Ph.D.
with Clint Twist and Edward Horton

2 If additional authors are named on the title page, include them in the citation with the same wording.

1 The author of the book "with" other authors.

NATIONAL GEOGRAPHIC
WASHINGTON, D.C.

4 Publication information

　　1　　　　　　　　　　　　2　　　　　　　　　3
Stewart, Robert, with Clint Twist, and Edward Horton. *Mysteries of History*.
　　　　　　4
　　Washington, DC: National Geographic Society, 2003. Print.

Figure A.3. A citation for a book by an author "with" others. Reprinted with permission of the National Geographic Society from the book *Mysteries of History* by Robert Stewart, Ph.D. Copyright ©2003 National Geographic.

A Citation for a Book by an Unidentified Author

- Sometimes not all the information needed for a citation is on the title page. The copyright page is the next place to look for publication information. However, if the author's name or editor's name is not printed on the title page, skip that part of the citation and go on to the next citation element.

- In this case the citation is a simple one. Skip the author's name because it is not on the title page and begin the citation with the title of the book.

CITATION BASICS:

- When the author or editor's name is not given on the title page, the information is skipped. When other information is missing, however, the *MLA* Handbook specifies abbreviations to indicate that the information is not available.

no publisher	N.p.
no city of publication	N.p.
no date	n.d.
no page numbers	n.pag.

A Citation for a Book by an Unidentified Author

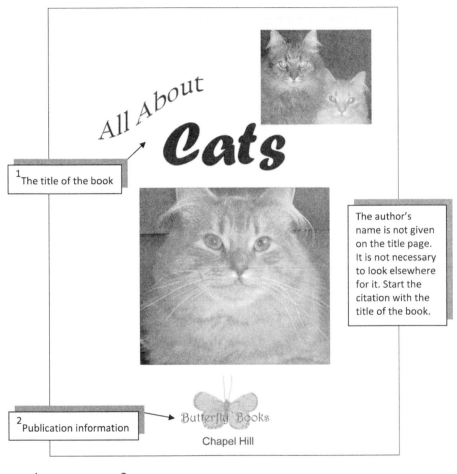

1   2
All about Cats. Chapel Hill: Butterfly, 2009.

Figure A.4. A citation for a book by an unidentified author. Used with permission.

A Citation for a Book by an Author with a Title

❏ The author of this book has both a title and a degree. Neither is ever considered part of his name and is not included in the citation.

CITATION BASICS:

- A suffix *is* part of an author's name. Be careful not to confuse a title or degree with a suffix.
- A suffix always comes after the author's name.

Examples of Titles Do *Not* Include in a Citation	Examples of Suffixes *Do* Include in a Citation
Ph. D., M.A., Ed.D., M.F.A.	Jr. or Sr.
Professor Emeritus	II, III, IV (any Roman numeral)
Doctor, M.D.	
Sir, Lady, Sister	
Senator, President, Mayor, etc.	

A CITATION FOR A BOOK BY AN AUTHOR WITH A TITLE

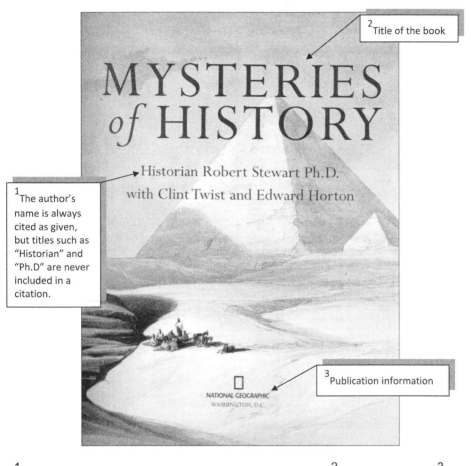

2 Title of the book

1 The author's name is always cited as given, but titles such as "Historian" and "Ph.D" are never included in a citation.

3 Publication information

1   2   3

Stewart, Robert, with Clint Twist, and Edward Horton. *Mysteries of History*. Washington,

    DC: National Geographic Society, 2003. Print.

Figure A.5. A citation for a book by an author with a title. Reprinted with permission of the National Geographic Society from the book *Mysteries of History* by Robert Stewart, Ph.D. Copyright ©2003 National Geographic.

A Citation for a Book with a Subtitle

- The subtitle of a book is usually located under the title. It is often in smaller print and may also be in a different font.

- If the subtitle is present on the title page, it should be included in the citation, even if it is long.

- The title is followed by a colon (:) and a space and then the entire subtitle, like this: Title: Subtitle

- Italicize the title and the subtitle.

CITATION BASICS:

- If the title ends with its own punctuation, like a question mark or an exclamation point (as in the example title page), omit the colon.
- If the subtitle ends with its own punctuation (like a question mark or exclamation point) omit the period at the end.
- Be sure to capitalize the first word of the subtitle and all subsequent words according to standard capitalization rules.

A CITATION FOR A BOOK WITH A SUBTITLE

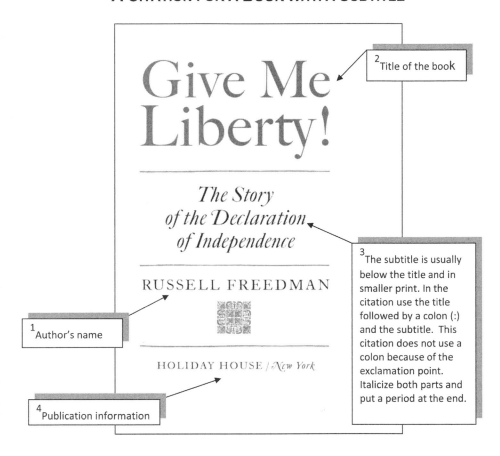

Freedman, Russell. *Give Me Liberty! The Story of the Declaration of Independence.*
New York: Holiday, 2000. Print.

Figure A.6. A citation for a book with a subtitle. Reprinted with permission.

A Citation for a Book That Is an Edition

- If a book includes an edition designation on the title page, it must be included in the citation.

- A Revised Edition is abbreviated as Rev. ed.

- If the edition is given a number, such as Second Edition or Third Edition, always use numbers to designate the edition, such as 2nd ed. or 3rd ed.

- An Abridged edition is abbreviated as Abr. ed.

- If the edition is identified by year, then it would be listed as 2009 ed.

- Notice that the "e" in ed. is not capitalized in the citation.

CITATION BASICS:

- It is always important to include the edition information in a citation. Editions may vary greatly in content, and page numbers are rarely the same. Readers would have a hard time finding the information used by the researcher if they did not know the correct edition.

- Notice that the edition information "to include new low-fat and vegetarian recipes" is not included in the citation. It is very unusual for edition information to be so long and descriptive. As long as the writer is sure that the citation information will send the reader to the correct source, it is permissible to omit extraneous information. Sometimes common sense must prevail.

A CITATION FOR A BOOK THAT IS AN EDITION

3 This book is a revised and expanded edition. This means that it has been published before, but this time it has been changed and more material has been added. It is important to designate the edition in a citation.

2 Title of the book

4 Publication information

1 Author's name

| 1 | 2 | 3 | 4 |
Christian, Rebecca. *Cooking the Spanish Way*. Rev. and exp. ed. Minneapolis: Lerner,

2002. Print.

Figure A.7. A citation for a book that is an edition. *Cooking the Spanish Way* by Rebecca Christian. Copyright © 2002 by Lerner Publications Company. Reprinted with the permission of Lerner Publications Company, a division of Lerner Publishing Group, Inc. All rights reserved. No part of this text excerpt may be used or reproduced in any manner whatsoever without the prior written permission of Lerner Publishing Group, Inc. Photograph by Tor Eigeland (http://www.toreigeland.com) used with permission.

A Citation for a Graphic Narrative

❑ Graphic narratives are becoming increasingly popular and offer students a wide array of material that can be used in research.

❑ Because of the importance of the graphic element in these books, many are a collaborative effort of two or more people. It is important to include all of the collaborators listed on the title page with their designated responsibilities.

CITATION BASICS:

- Notice that the name of the illustrator is included in the citation because this is a graphic work.
- If the illustrator were the subject of the student's research, that name would begin the citation.
- The publisher's imprint (Rosen Central) is hyphenated with the publishing house (Rosen) to specify how this book was published (see Figure A.10).

A Citation for a Graphic Narrative

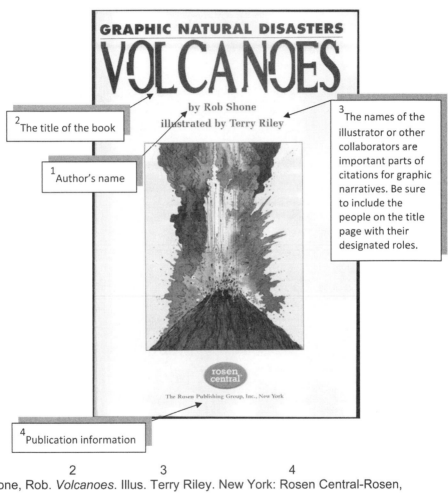

2 The title of the book

1 Author's name

3 The names of the illustrator or other collaborators are important parts of citations for graphic narratives. Be sure to include the people on the title page with their designated roles.

4 Publication information

1   2   3   4

Shone, Rob. *Volcanoes*. Illus. Terry Riley. New York: Rosen Central-Rosen,

2007. Print.

Figure A.8. A citation for a graphic narrative. From: *Volcanoes* by Rob Shone, copyright 2007 by The Rosen Publishing Group, 29 East 21st Street, New York, NY, 10010, and reprinted with permission.

A Citation for a Book with More Than One City of Publication

❑ Knowing where a book was published helps to identify the book and answer the question "How was it published?"

❑ The rule is simple: Always use the first city given.

❑ It is never necessary to use a state or country after the city.

CITATION BASICS:

- The publishing company is only identified by its unique name—in this case, Bulfinch. Words such as *Press, Publishers, Company*, etc. are always omitted, as they are unnecessary.
- If the publisher is a university press, then it is identified by the school and the initials UP, as in Harvard UP.
- The subtitle of this book is located above the title, which is unusual but not unheard of. How do you know it is not the name of a series? A series name is always "larger" than the single book, so is often plural, as the examples A.7, A.8, and A.10. A subtitle always makes more sense read after the primary title, as in *Photocraft: Cool Things to Do with the Pictures You Love.*

A Citation for a Book with More Than

One City of Publication

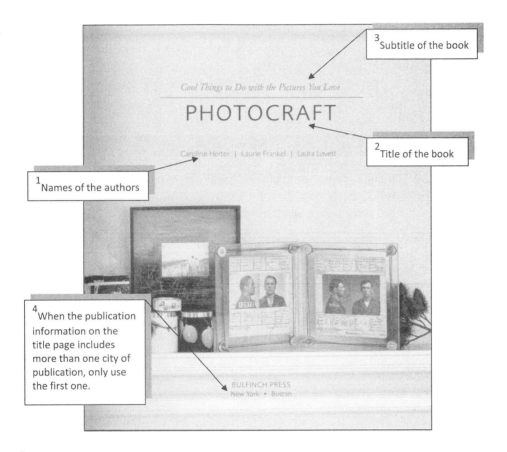

1
Herter, Caroline, Laurie Frankel, and Laura Lovett. *Photocraft: Cool Things to Do with*
4
the Pictures You Love. New York: Bulfinch, 2005. Print.

Figure A.9. A citation for a book with more than one city of publication. From: *PHOTOCRAFT: Cool Things to Do with the Pictures You Love* by Laurie Frankel, published by Little, Brown, & Company, used with permission.

A Citation for a Book with a Publisher's Imprint

❑ Many books are published with a publisher's imprint. Including the imprint information in the citation helps answer the question, "How was it published?"

❑ If a publisher's imprint is included on the title page, list it first with a hyphen and then the name of the publishing house, as in the example:

Benchmark-Marshall Cavendish

CITATIONS BASICS:

- In citations, the names of publishing companies do not include words like *company, publishers, books, press,* or *incorporated.* Include only the name that identifies the publisher.

A CITATION FOR A BOOK WITH A PUBLISHER'S IMPRINT

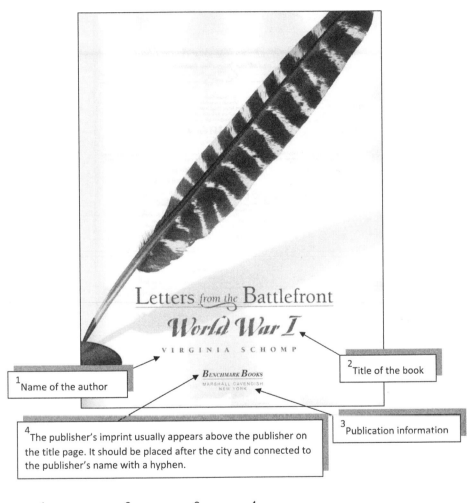

Schomp, Virginia. *World War I*. New York: Benchmark- Marshall Cavendish, 2004. Print.

Figure A.10. A citation for a book with a publisher's imprint. Reprinted by permission of Marshall Cavendish.

A Citation for a Book with More Than One Copyright Date

☐ It is not uncommon to see more than one date on the copyright page. Use the most recent copyright date for the citation.

CITATION BASICS:

- However, the date used must be a copyright date. If there is a statement that says something like "reprinted in," with a date, do not use that date. Use the date of the copyright.
- A book receives a new copyright date when changes have been made to the text that are substantive. Those changes make the work "new" and original, thus, a new copyright. A reprint, on the other hand, is just that—another press run.

A Citation for a Book with More Than One Copyright Date

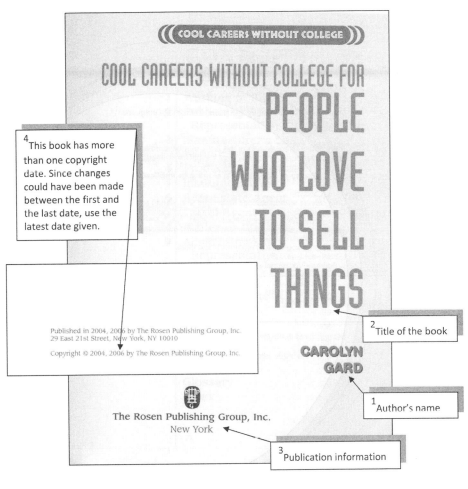

4 This book has more than one copyright date. Since changes could have been made between the first and the last date, use the latest date given.

Published in 2004, 2006 by The Rosen Publishing Group, Inc.
29 East 21st Street, New York, NY 10010

Copyright © 2004, 2006 by The Rosen Publishing Group, Inc.

2 Title of the book

CAROLYN GARD

1 Author's name

The Rosen Publishing Group, Inc.
New York

3 Publication information

1   2   3
Gard, Carolyn. *Cool Careers without College for People Who Love to Sell Things*. New
        4
   York: Rosen, 2006. Print.

Figure A.11. A citation for a book with more than one copyright date. From: *Cool Careers without College for People Who Love to Sell Things* by Carolyn Gard, copyright 2006 by The Rosen Group, 29 East 21st Street, New York, NY, 10010, and reprinted with permission.

A Citation for a Book with an Editor

❑ An edited book is cited just as an authored book is. The only difference is that the editor's name is followed by a comma and the abbreviation "ed."

CITATION BASICS:

- If the editor's name includes a middle initial, both the period and the comma are included before the abbreviation "ed." For example, Smith, John T., ed.
- There are all types of edited books. Sometimes it is appropriate to cite the entire book, as illustrated here. At other times, it is appropriate to cite only a selection in a book, as illustrated in Figure A.13. At other times, it is necessary to use cross-referencing, as illustrated in Figure A.14. How do you know when to use each type of citation?
  - Sometimes an editor is given on the title page, but no individual authors are listed for articles or chapters in the book. If this is the case the researcher should cite the entire book and include page numbers at the end of the citation if only a certain section of the book was used.
  - Cite only the selection used if the writer has chosen only one chapter, article, short story, or poem from an edited book.
  - Use cross-referencing (Figure A.14) if two or more selections from an edited book of various authors are used.

A Citation for a Book with an Editor

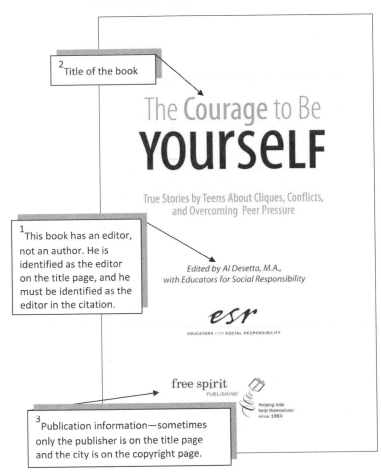

²Title of the book

The Courage to Be **YOURSELF**

True Stories by Teens About Cliques, Conflicts, and Overcoming Peer Pressure

¹This book has an editor, not an author. He is identified as the editor on the title page, and he must be identified as the editor in the citation.

Edited by Al Desetta, M.A., with Educators for Social Responsibility

esr

EDUCATORS FOR SOCIAL RESPONSIBILITY

free spirit
PUBLISHING

Helping kids help themselves since 1983

³Publication information—sometimes only the publisher is on the title page and the city is on the copyright page.

1   2
Desetta, Al, ed., with Educators for Social Responsibility. *The Courage to Be Yourself:*

True Stories by Teens about Cliques, Conflicts, and Overcoming Peer Pressure.
      3
Minneapolis: Free Spirit, 2005. Print.

Figure A.12. A citation for a book with an editor. Reprinted with permission from Free Spirit Publishing.

A Citation for a Selection in an Edited Book

❑ In this case the citation is for one poem because that is all that was used by the writer. The citation begins with the name of the poet (author) and is followed by the title of the poem in quotation marks because it is a selection in the book.

❑ The remainder of the citation comes from the title page. The title of the book comes next. Italicize it, as always. End with a period.

❑ Follow the title of the book with the editor or editors, preceded by Ed. or Eds.

❑ If there is any other information on the title page, such as edition, or volume number, it comes next in this order:

   ❑ Edition

   ❑ Volume number

❑ The publication information comes next.

❑ Follow the publication information with the page numbers of the piece. Do not use p. or pp.

❑ End with the designation, "Print."

CITATION BASICS:

- When a specific selection is cited in a book, the author and the selection must come first, followed by the title of the larger work. Follow the book title with the name of the editor. When the editor's name appears in this position instead of the beginning of the citation, it is preceded with *Ed.* or *Eds.* (with a capital E).
- The editor of this book is not a specific person, but an agency. It is treated the same as a person in a citation.
- Notice that the number in the title remains a numeral.

A Citation for a Selection in an Edited Book

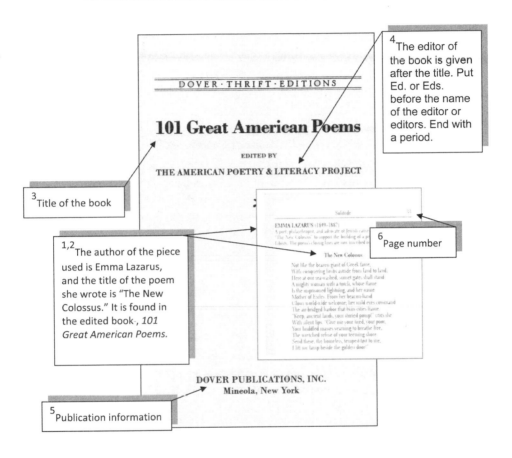

4 The editor of the book is given after the title. Put Ed. or Eds. before the name of the editor or editors. End with a period.

3 Title of the book

1,2 The author of the piece used is Emma Lazarus, and the title of the poem she wrote is "The New Colossus." It is found in the edited book, *101 Great American Poems.*

6 Page number

5 Publication information

> 1   2   3   4
> Lazarus, Emma. "The New Colossus." *101 Great American Poems*. Ed. The American
>   5   6
>   Poetry and Literacy Project. Mineola: Dover, 1998. 33. Print.

Figure A.13. A citation for a selection in an edited book. Reprinted with permission from Dover Publications, Inc.

Citations for Two or More Selections in an Edited Book (Cross-References)

❏ If a writer uses information from two or more selections in an edited book, it is common to use a type of citation known as cross-referencing. Cross-referencing lets the writer make one citation for the book and then add abbreviated citations for the specific selections used.

❏ The abbreviated references (cross-references) only cite the author, the piece, the editor of the book, and page numbers.

CITATION BASICS:

- Sometimes it is necessary to do a little investigative reading to know what type of book a student is using. In this case, the title is the clue. It does not make any sense unless you know that *Guys Read* is a Web site. The introduction of the book reveals this information.

- A book title (or any other title that is usually italicized) within a book title is not italicized. The absence of the italics where it would normally be tells the reader that he is looking at a title within a title, as in the example. Another example would be, *A Critical Reading of* The Scarlet Letter.

- However, if the title of a book includes a title that is normally in quotation marks, such as the title of a poem or short story, the book title is entirely italicized and the poem or short story title is enclosed in quotation marks as it would normally be. For example, *A Psychological Deconstruction of Edgar Alan Poe's "The Raven"*.

CITATIONS FOR TWO OR MORE SELECTIONS IN AN EDITED BOOK

(CROSS-REFERENCES)

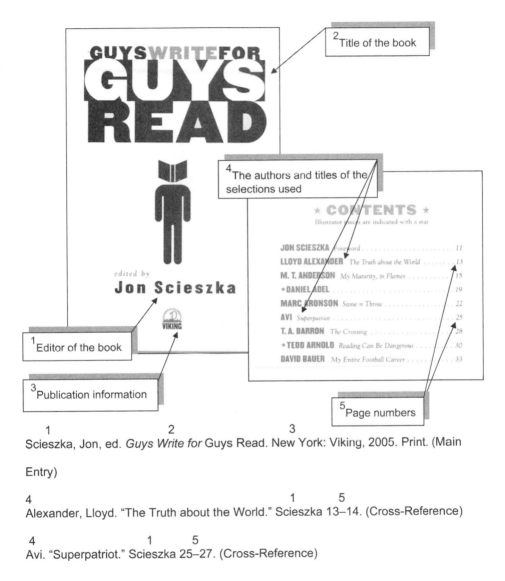

²Title of the book

⁴The authors and titles of the selections used

¹Editor of the book

³Publication information

⁵Page numbers

1	2	3

Scieszka, Jon, ed. *Guys Write for* Guys Read. New York: Viking, 2005. Print. (Main Entry)

4		1	5

Alexander, Lloyd. "The Truth about the World." Scieszka 13–14. (Cross-Reference)

4		1	5

Avi. "Superpatriot." Scieszka 25–27. (Cross-Reference)

Figure A.14. Citations for two or more selections in an edited book (cross-references). From: *Guys Write for* Guys Read, edited by Jon Scieszka, copyright © 2005 by Jon Scieszka, selection and introduction. Used by permission of Viking Children's Books, A Division of Penguin Young Readers Group, A Member of Penguin Group (USA) Inc., 345 Hudson Street, New York, NY 10014. All rights reserved.

A Citation for an Unsigned Selection in a Multivolume Set

◻ Students often use books that are parts of multivolume sets. Many of these books are reference books. Reference books are not cited differently because they are reference books. What influences the citation is that they are part of a multivolume set.

◻ Sometimes books in a multivolume set are identified by volume numbers, and sometimes each book has its own title. Sometimes they have both. This example uses a book that has only a volume number.

CITATION BASICS:	
Citation Creation Question	**MLA Citation Answer**
Who wrote the information used?	• Not given—begin with the title of the selection
What did the author write?	• Title of the selection, in quotation marks
Where is the piece found?	• Title of the multivolume set, italicized • Name of the editor (if on title page) preceded by *Ed.* • Edition (if information is on title page) • Number of the volume (if on title page) preceded by *Vol.*
How was it published?	• City: Publisher, Copyright date • Page numbers • *Print* designation

A CITATION FOR AN UNSIGNED SELECTION IN A

MULTIVOLUME SET

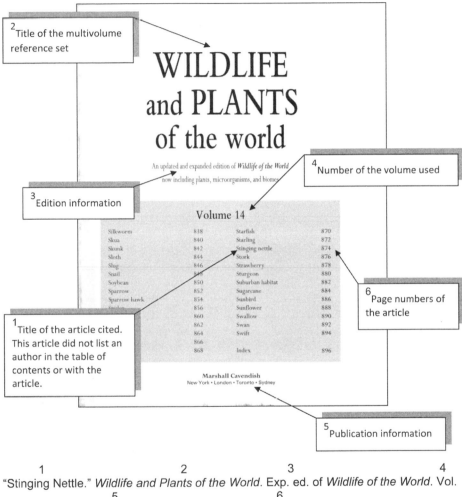

1
"Stinging Nettle." *Wildlife and Plants of the World*. Exp. ed. of *Wildlife of the World*. Vol.

5 6
14. New York: Marshall Cavendish, 1999. 874–75. Print.

Figure A.15. A citation for an unsigned selection in a multivolume set. Reprinted with permission from Marshall Cavendish.

A Citation for a Signed Selection in a Multivolume Set

- ❑ In many reference books, the author's name, if it is given, is found in small type at the end of the selection. If it is not there or at the beginning of the selection, the writer can be satisfied that the author's name is not available.

- ❑ If the author's name is available, the citation begins with it.

- ❑ The title of the selection is enclosed in quotation marks. The period is inside the quotation marks.

- ❑ The title page of the book has the title of the multivolume set. Underline it and end with a period.

- ❑ Follow the title with the name of the editor if it is given. Begin with *Ed.* or *Eds.* and the name of the editor or editors in the order given.

- ❑ If there is any other information on the title page, such as edition, or volume number, it comes next in this order:

  - ❑ Edition

  - ❑ Volume number

- ❑ The publication information comes next.

- ❑ End with the page numbers of the article. Do not use *p.* or *pp.*

CITATION BASICS:

- If the title page of the volume has both the title of the multivolume set and an individual title for that specific volume, see the example in Figure A.17.

A Citation for a Signed Selection in a Multivolume Set

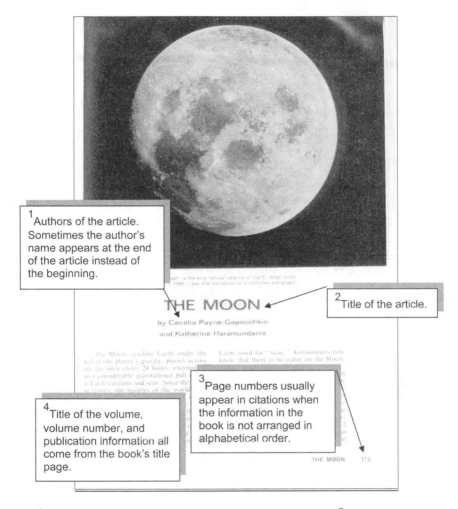

1 Authors of the article. Sometimes the author's name appears at the end of the article instead of the beginning.

THE MOON

by Cecelia Payne-Gaposchkin
and Katherine Haramundanis

2 Title of the article.

3 Page numbers usually appear in citations when the information in the book is not arranged in alphabetical order.

4 Title of the volume, volume number, and publication information all come from the book's title page.

1   2

Payne-Gaposchkin, Cecilia, and Katherine Haramundanis. "The Moon." *The New Book*

4   3

of Popular Science. Vol. 1. New York: Scholastic, 2008. 113–26. Print.

Figure A.16. A citation for a signed selection in a multivolume set. Copyright ©2008 by Scholastic, Inc. All rights reserved. Used with permission. Picture by NASA.

A Citation for a Titled Volume in a Multivolume Set

❏ Sometimes volumes in a set are identified by titles instead of numbers. In this case the volume has both a title and a number.

❏ If no author name is given, the citation begins with the title of the article used.

CITATION BASICS:

- Citation elements for an individually titled volume in a multivolume set:

Citation Creation Question	MLA Citation Answer
Who wrote the information used?	• Author's name (if given)
What did the author write?	• Title of the article used in quotation marks
Where is the piece found?	• Title of the individual volume • Name of the editor (if on title page) preceded by *Ed.* • Edition (if information is on title page)
How was it published?	• City: Publisher, Copyright date • Page numbers • *Print* designation

- If desired, the citation can include additional information about the multivolume set, as shown below:

Harris, Nancy. *Chemistry*. Vero Beach: Rourke, 2008. Print. Vol. 5 of *Rourke's World of Science Encyclopedia*.

A CITATION FOR A TITLED VOLUME IN A MULTIVOLUME SET

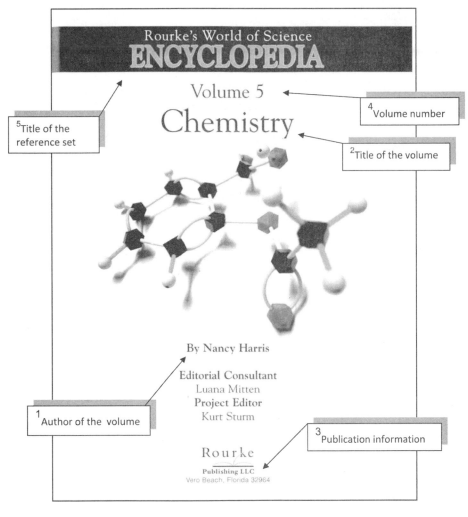

1   2   3

Harris, Nancy. *Chemistry*. Vero Beach: Rourke, 2008. Print.

Figure A.17. A citation for a titled volume in a multivolume set. Used with permission from Rourke Publishing, LLC.

A Citation for a Signed Encyclopedia Article

- A general encyclopedia is one that includes a wide array of articles on multiple topics. A specialized encyclopedia covers a narrow range of topics, such as plants and animals, diseases, American history, etc. Specialized encyclopedias are considered multivolume reference books, even if the word "encyclopedia" is part of the title. Citations for those sources must be complete (see Figures A 15, 16, and 17).

- General encyclopedias are cited with abbreviated citations.

- As with many other reference books, the author's name is often at the end of the article in very small type.

- The title of the article must be written exactly as it appears in the article.

- Italicize the title of the encyclopedia.

- End with the designation, "Print."

CITATION BASICS:

- Any article title, whether in an encyclopedia or other book, must be written exactly as it appears. For example, an entry for Edgar Alan Poe would appear as Poe, Edgar Alan. In the citation it would be written as "Poe, Edgar Alan."

- It is never necessary to include the volume number or page numbers since general encyclopedias are always arranged in alphabetical order.

- Full publication information is not included in a citation for a general encyclopedia—just the abbreviated edition information.

A Citation for a Signed Encyclopedia Article

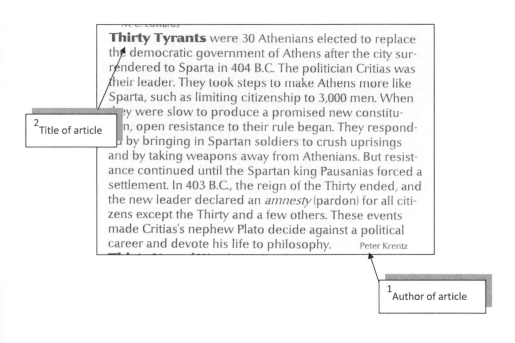

Krentz, Peter. "Thirty Tyrants." *World Book Encyclopedia*. 2009 ed. Print.

Figure A.18. A citation for a signed encyclopedia article. Krentz, Peter. "Thirty Tyrants." *The World Book Encyclopedia*. ©2008. World Book, Inc. By permission of the publisher. http://www.worldbookonline.com. All rights reserved.

A Citation for an Unsigned Encyclopedia Article

- ❑ Look for an author at the end of the article. If an author's name is not given, then the title of the entry comes first.

- ❑ The title of the article must be written exactly as it appears in the article and must be in quotation marks.

- ❑ Italicize the title of the encyclopedia.

- ❑ Omit full publication information and only use the abbreviated edition information.

- ❑ End with the designation, "Print."

A Citation for an Unsigned Encyclopedia Article

1 Title of the article

QUETZAL. For gorgeous plumage few birds surpass the quetzal. Found in rain forests from southern Mexico to Bolivia, the quetzal was the sacred bird of the ancient Mayas and Aztecs; today it is the national emblem of Guatemala. The male resplendent quetzal is adorned with a blue-green train that is 2 feet (0.6 meter) long—nearly twice as long as his body. His head has a rounded hairlike crest. His head and breast are brilliant gold-green, his back is blue with a curly gold-tinged mantle, and his belly is crimson. Quetzals belong to the genus *Pharomacrus* of the trogon family, Trogonidae. The resplendent quetzal is *Pharomacrus mocino*. (*See also* Birds.)

No author is given for the article

1
"Quetzal." *Compton's Encyclopedia.* 2005 ed. Print.

Figure A.19. A citation for an unsigned encyclopedia article. Reprinted from *Compton's Encyclopedia*, 2005 ed. Used with permission from Encyclopaedia Britannica.

A Citation for a Dictionary Entry

- A citation for a dictionary entry is very similar to a citation for an unsigned encyclopedia.

- The citation begins with the entry that the student used, in quotation marks.

- The title of the dictionary comes next, italicized.

- The edition of the dictionary follows the title.

- The final item is the year of publication.

CITATION BASICS:

- These examples apply to general dictionaries only. If the dictionary used is a specialized dictionary (e.g. a science dictionary), then full publication information from the title page should be included in the citation. It would look similar to this:

"Entry." *Title of dictionary*. Editor's name (preceded by the abbreviation Ed.).

Edition. City: Publisher, date. Print.

- The second example applies when there is more than one entry for a word ([2]zany), and when there is more than one definition for the entry (Def. 2.). Specify the entry and the definition with the same designation that the publisher uses.

A Citation for a Dictionary Entry

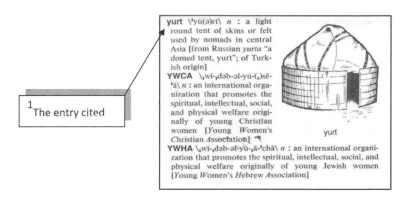

1
"Yurt." *Merriam-Webster's Intermediate Dictionary.* Rev. ed. 2004. Print.

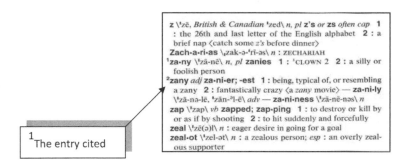

1
"²Zany." Def. 2. *Merriam-Webster's Intermediate Dictionary.* Rev. ed. 2004. Print.

Figure A.20. A citation for a dictionary entry. By permission. From *Merriam-Webster's Intermediate Dictionary* ©2004 by Merriam-Webster, Incorporated (www.Merriam-Webster.com).

Appendix B:
Examples of Citations for Periodicals

A Citation for an Article in a Magazine

- Begin with the name of the author, inverted. End with a period.

- Put the title of the article in quotation marks. Enclose the final period in the quotation marks.

- Italicize the name of the magazine. Do *not* end with a period.

- Follow the magazine name with the date of publication—first the day (if it is a weekly magazine), month, then the year. Use the month abbreviations in the chart below.

- Follow the date with a colon and a space.

- Next come the page numbers and a period. Hyphenate the page numbers if they are consecutive, and use a + if they are nonconsecutive as in 5+.

- End with the medium of the source, "Print."

CITATION BASICS:

- Unlike books, magazines do not have a "standard" spot like a title page or copyright page where writers can find the information they need to create citations. Sometimes the date of the magazine can be the hardest piece of information to find. It may be at the bottom of each page, on the table of contents page, on the cover, or on the spine of the magazine.

- The title of the magazine is not enough to help the reader find the article cited. The reader must also know the date of publication and page numbers. A colon separates the date from the page numbers, and a period is placed after the page numbers. Never use *p.* or *pp.*

- Abbreviate the months of the year except May, June, and July

Month	Abbreviation	Month	Abbreviation
January	Jan.	July	July
February	Feb.	August	Aug.
March	Mar.	September	Sept.
April	Apr.	October	Oct.
May	May	November	Nov.
June	June	December	Dec.

A CITATION FOR AN ARTICLE IN A MAGAZINE

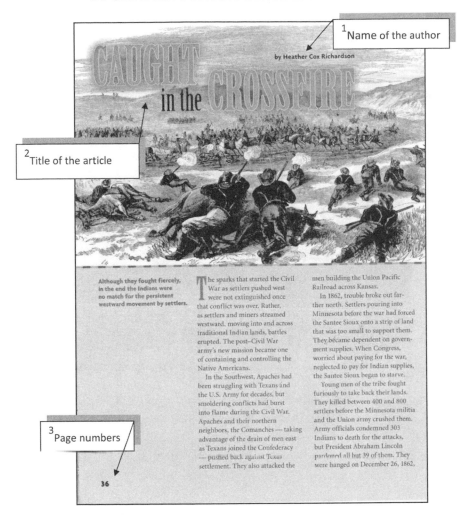

1
Name of the author

2
Title of the article

3
Page numbers

1   2   3
Richardson, Heather Cox. "Caught in the Crossfire." *Cobblestone* Jan. 2009: 36–37.

Print.

Figure B.1. A citation for an article in a magazine. From COBBLESTONE's January 2009 issue: The West and the Civil War, © 2009, Carus Publishing Company, published by Cobblestone Publishing, 30 Grove Street, Suite C, Peterborough, NH 03458. All Rights Reserved. Used by permission of the publisher. Picture credit: North Winds Picture Archives. Used with permission.

A Citation for an Article in a Journal

- A journal citation begins as other citations do—with the author's name first.

- The article name follows in quotation marks with the period enclosed.

- Italicize the title of the journal but *do not* end with a period because the journal is not yet completely identified.

- Follow the title of the journal with the volume number and issue number, if present. In the example the journal is number 89. That information is usually on the cover or the table of contents page. It is followed by the year in parentheses.

- Put a colon after the year and end with the page numbers. If the article is printed on consecutive pages use a dash between the first page number and the last. If the page numbers are not consecutive, use a + as in the example.

- End with the medium of the source, "Print."

CITATION BASICS:

- The title of this journal article includes the title of another publication, *A Nation at Risk,* as indicated by the italic type. Sometimes a little investigative work is needed to know how to handle a title within a title. Google quickly informs us that this particular title is a government report; therefore, it is italicized.

A Citation for an Article in a Journal

Teacher Professionalism Since *A Nation at Risk*

²Title of the article

The story of a recently burned-out high school English teacher confirms the finding ...ed in *A Nation at Risk* that "the professional working life of teachers is on the ...nacceptable." It appears that not much has improved in the past 25 years.

¹Authors of the article

BY MICHAEL P. GRADY, KRISTINE C. HELBLING, AND DENNIS R. LUBECK

HOW MANY times have you seen a sweatshirt emblazoned with "If your house hasn't collapsed, thank an architect" or "Fair divorce settlements couldn't happen without your lawyer"? Lawyers and architects don't need silk-screened slogans to remind the public of their worth; their value to the community is measured by the fees they collect and the respect they receive. Teachers, though they're expected to be martyrs to the cause of children and are required to continually develop themselves professionally, get no such respect. In its place, they get limited autonomy and a fraction of the salaries of other professionals. No wonder teachers need a bumper sticker to remind us all: "If you can read this, thank a teacher."

While the definition of professionalism can be elusive and its elements are subject to debate, some features would be common to any definition. For one, the public accords a certain respect to professionals because of their special skills and knowledge. Professionals exercise discretion in making decisions within the scope of their expertise, and they assume some authority for their own professional development.

Are teachers professionals, and, if so... Certainly, principals, superintendents, de... and officials in state departments of educ... siderable input into defining the autho...

⁴ page number of the article

■ *MICHAEL P. GRADY is a prof... cational Studies at St. Louis Universi... is a reference and subject librarian for ...ington University in St. Louis. DENN... the International Education Consortium in St. Louis.*

³Date of the journal

...hool and the scho... ...determine how professionalism ...rceive an erosion of their pro... *Nation at Risk* appeared, and they ...h accelerating since No Child Left Behind.

Image: Stockbyte/Artville

APRIL 2008   603

¹
Grady, Michael P., Kristine C. Helbling, and Dennis R. Lubeck. "Teacher
²   ³   ⁴
Professionalism since *A Nation at Risk*." *Phi Delta Kappan* 89.8 (2008): 603+.

Print.

Figure B.2. A citation for an article in a journal. Reprinted with permission from Phi Delta Kappan International.

A Citation for a Newspaper Article

- Begin the citation with the author of the article.

- Put the title of the article in quotation marks. End with a period inside the quotation marks.

- Italicize the title of the newspaper. If the title begins with *The,* do not include it in the citation, as in the example.

- The complete date comes next with the month abbreviated, as appropriate.

- Include the edition if one is identified on the masthead.

- Place a colon after the edition or date (if there is no edition)

- Follow the same guidelines for page numbers as those that apply to magazines and journals. If an article continues to the next page, use a hyphen between the page numbers. If it skips to another page, use a +. The article in the example continues on page 3. Since it begins on the first page, a + is used.

- If the newspaper is divided into sections, then the section designation must accompany the page number.

- End with the medium of the source, "Print."

CITATION BASICS:

- If the city is not included in the title of the newspaper, put it after the title in brackets. For example, if the title of this newspaper were *The News,* it would appear like this in the citation: *News* [Greenville]

A Citation for a Newspaper Article

1	2	3	4

Davidson, Paul. "Dramatic Utility Bill Increase Expected." *Greenville News* 16 June

5

2008, final ed.: A1+. Print.

Figure B.3. A citation for a newspaper article. Used with permission from
The Greenville News.

Appendix C:
Examples of Citations for Computer Sources

A Citation for an Article in an Online Encyclopedia

- This citation is for an article in Wikipedia. The article is not signed so the citation begins with the title of the article.

- The title of the article is enclosed in quotation marks.

- The title of the site is in italics, just as the title of a print encyclopedia would be.

- The sponsor of the site is given next if it is available. If it is not, use the designation *N.p.*

- Date of publication or date of last update is next. In this case there is a updated posting date.

- The medium identifier, *Web*, is next, followed by the date of access.

CITATION BASICS:

- The *MLA Handbook* prescribes that the publisher or sponsor always be included in a citation if the information is available. If not, the designation N.p. is used.

A Citation for an Article in an Online Encyclopedia

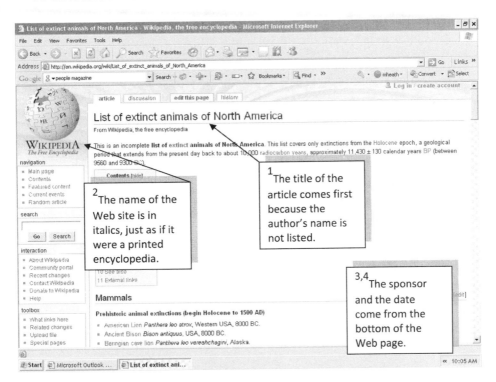

1   2   3   4

"List of Extinct Animals of North America." *Wikipedia.* Wikimedia, 20 Apr. 2009.

     Web. 24 Apr. 2009.

Figure C.1. A citation for an article in an online encyclopedia. Used with permission.

A Citation for a Web Page

- Think of citing a Web page as if it were an article in a magazine. It is part of the larger whole—the Web site. The concept is the same, and the citations are very similar.

- If there is an author or editor, that person's name should come first.

- The title of the page is in quotations, just as if it were an article in a periodical.

- The title of the site is italicized because it is the entire publication, just as if it were the title of a magazine.

- If there is a sponsoring agency (such as NASA in this example), that information is next.

- List the date the site was last updated or a copyright date if that information is available. If a date is not available, use the designation *n.d.*

- End with the medium identification, "Web," and the date the student accessed the information.

CITATION BASICS:

- Sometimes, as with this example, the sponsoring agency is clearly visible and lends a great deal to the credibility of the site. If there is no publisher or sponsor, use the designation *N.p.*

A Citation for a Web Page

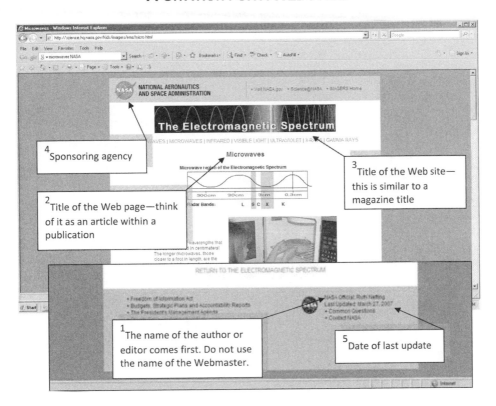

```
  1                    2                    3              4        5
Netting, Ruth, ed. "Microwaves." The Electromagnetic Spectrum. NASA, 27 Mar 2007.

   Web. 18 June 2009.
```

Figure C.2. A citation for a Web page. Used with permission.

A Citation for a Web Site

- Sometimes a student takes information from several pages in a Web site, just as he might use several chapters in a book. When this is the case, it is appropriate to write the citation for the entire site. Since the Web pages form a cohesive, whole site, the entire site should be cited.

- If there is the name of the person who is responsible for the content of the site, use that person's name as the author or editor. Do not use the name of the Webmaster.

- Italicize the title of the Web site.

- Use the name of the publisher or sponsor next. If none is given, use the designation *N.p.*

- Put the date of posting or last update. If both dates are given, use the date of last update.

- End with the medium identification of "Web," and the date the student accessed the site.

A CITATION FOR A WEB SITE

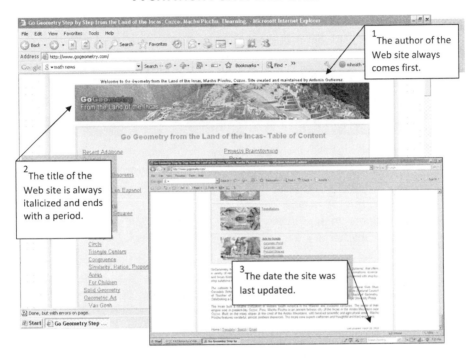

Gutierrez, Antonio. *Go Geometry: From the Land of the Incas.* N.p. 22 Mar. 2009. Web.

24 Mar. 2009.

Figure C.3. A citation for a Web site. Used with permission.

A Citation for an Article on a Wiki

- Entries in wikis, as a rule, are not signed, so the citation begins with the title of the entry, enclosed in quotation marks.

- The title of the wiki is italicized and followed by a period.

- The publisher or sponsor comes next. If that information is not available, use the designation *N.p.*

- The date of the posting, if available, or the copyright date comes next.

- The last part of the citation is the medium identifier, *Web,* and the date the student accessed the information from the site.

CITATION BASICS:

- The *MLA Handbook* calls for the inclusion of the sponsor, if there is one identified on the Web site. This information is often not evident to students and is sometimes hard to find. Often the best place to look is the home page.

- Sometimes, as in this case, the title of the wiki and the sponsor, or publisher, are the same. List the title in both positions in the citation.

A Citation for an Article on a Wiki

1   2   2
"How to Raise Butterflies." *Wikihow*. Wikihow, n.d. Web. 2 March 2009.

Figure C.4. A citation for an article on a wiki. Used with permission.

123

A Citation for a Blog or Discussion Board Entry

- Begin with the author's name and follow it with a period.

- Follow the author's name with the title of the blog entry. Enclose in quotation marks and end with a period inside the quotation marks.

- Italicize the title of the Web site if there is a title different than that of the blog entry.

- Next list the name of the publisher or sponsor of the site. If none is given, use the designation *N.p.*

- Next insert the date of the posting followed by a period. If no date is given, use the designation *n.d.*

- Finish with the medium identifier *Web* and the date of access.

CITATION BASICS:

- Sometimes it is necessary to include the URL of a Web site to completely identify it. The *MLA Handbook* discourages the use of long URLs if it is possible for them to be shortened. If the URL does not fit on one line of the citation, it should be divided at a /. If there is a search page, use its URL.
- Be sure to enclose the URL in angle brackets < > with a period at the end.

A CITATION FOR A BLOG OR DISCUSSION BOARD ENTRY

1 2
Gertz, Emily. "Can Offshore Drilling Lower Gas Prices, Make the U.S. Energy
3 4 5
Independent?" *Stop Global Warming*. Change.org, 5 Oct. 2008. Web. 2 Mar.

2009.

Figure C.5. A citation for a blog or discussion board entry. Used with permission.

A Citation for an Article in an Online Periodical

- ❏ Online periodical articles are cited much the same way as print periodical articles. Students can create one if they know how to create the other.

- ❏ Begin with the name of the author.

- ❏ Put quotation marks around the title of the article.

- ❏ Italicize the name of the periodical.

- ❏ Next comes the name of the publisher or sponsor and the date of the article. If there is no publisher or sponsor, use *N.p.* If there is no date use *n.d.*

- ❏ End with the medium identifier, "Web," and the date of access.

CITATION BASICS:

- Sometimes, as is the case with this example, the name of the periodical and the name of the publisher or sponsor are the same. Students can have trouble spotting the name of the publisher. Help them look at the bottom of the page or on the home page to find the information they need.

A Citation for an Article in an Online Periodical

1   2   3   3

Borrell, Brendan. "Are Octopuses Smart?" *Scientific American.* Scientific American, 27
      4

Feb. 2009. Web. 3 Mar. 2009.

Figure C.6. A citation for an article in an online periodical. From http://www.sciam.
com/article.cfm?id=are-octopuses-smart. Copyright ©2009 by Scientific American,
Inc. All rights reserved. Photograph by Tim Treqenza, "Tregenaoctopus." http://
www.flickr.com. Used under terms of the Creative Commons Attribution 2.0
Generic License, http://creativecommons.org/licenses/by/2.0/deed.en

A Citation for Nonprint Material
on the Web

❏ Citations for nonprint Web sources are easy to create. Just follow the basic rules for other Web sources found in Appendix C and adjust them, as appropriate.

❏ In this example the student is studying the speeches of Dr. Martin Luther King, Jr. He has found a shortened video clip on a popular Web site. The citation starts with the author of the speech and the title.

❏ The name of the Web site is italicized.

❏ Because the video is a version of the speech, as opposed to the entire speech, that information needs to come next, followed by the person who posted it. This information is important because several people have posted similar videos, and the reader needs to know which one the student used.

❏ Now the citation ends the way most Web citations do—with the publisher or sponsor of the site, the date of posting, the designation of *Web*, and the date of access.

CITATION BASICS:

- The Web is full of images, videos, and audio files of all kinds. Using these materials helps engage students and also gives them vibrant insight into the topic they are studying. Citations for these sources are easy to create. Just apply the basic rules and some common sense.
- Remember to use the medium identification *Web* no matter what the material. In other words, if this video were viewed in class, the student would cite it as DVD, Videocassette, or whatever medium it was. Material from the Web, however, is always identified as *Web*.

A Citation for Nonprint Material on the Web

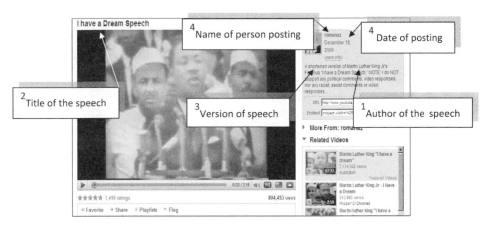

```
              1                    2                  3           4
King, Martin Luther, Jr. "I Have a Dream Speech." YouTube. Shortened vers. Posted
              5                    6
        by romanaz. Google, 18 Dec. 2006. Web. 19 Apr. 2009.
```

Figure C.7. A citation for nonprint material on the Web. Used with permission.

A Citation for an Online Scholarly Journal

- Some scholarly journals appear only in print, some only on the Web, and some appear in both media. In order to make it easy for students to cite materials accurately, it makes sense for them to cite the source that they are using. That means that they will not be concerned as to whether or not an online journal also appears in print.

- To cite an online scholarly journal, use the basic guidelines for a print journal.

- Begin with the author or authors, followed by the title of the article, in quotations.

- Italicize the name of the journal and follow that with the volume, issue (if given), and year, in parentheses, followed by a colon.

- Sometimes page numbers are available, but more often they are not. If not, use the designation, *n.p.*

- End with the medium identification, "Web," and date of access.

A CITATION FOR AN ONLINE SCHOLARLY JOURNAL

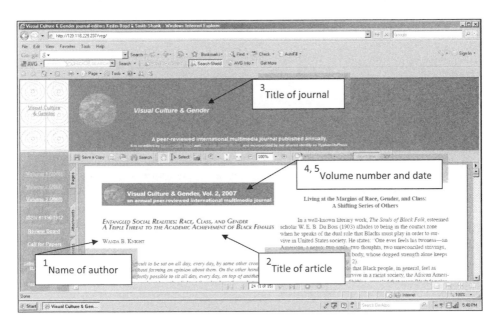

1   2
Knight, Wanda B. "Entangled Social Realities: Race, Class, and Gender a Triple Threat
                                                                3   4
to the Academic Achievement of Black Females." *Visual Culture and Gender* 2
        5
(2007): n.p. Web. 19 Apr. 2009.

Figure C.8. A citation for an online scholarly journal. Used with permission.

A Citation for an Article in an Online Database

- A citation for an article in an online database includes all the elements of the original print source and the elements of the online source as well. The citation always begins with the print source. This is to let readers know that the source is available in a medium that is generally available; many databases are available by subscription only.

- Citation elements 1 through 4 are written just as if the student were citing the print version of *Boys' Life.*

- Item 5 is the name of the database accessed.

- The citation ends with the identification of the medium, *Web,* and the date the student accessed the information.

CITATION BASICS:

- Many online subscription databases provide users with ready-made citations. These are usually not correct, however. Teachers and students need to be careful to check them before accepting their accuracy.

A CITATION FOR AN ARTICLE IN AN ONLINE DATABASE

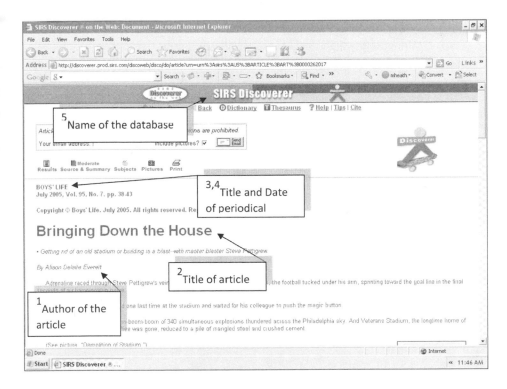

```
1                          2                        3          4     5
```
Everett, Alison Delsite. "Bringing Down the House." *Boys' Life*, July 2005. *SIRS*

Discoverer. Web. 18 Mar. 2009.

Figure C.9. A citation for an article in an online database. Image published with permission of ProQuest LLC. ©2009, ProQuest LLC; all rights reserved. Further reproduction is prohibited without permission.

A Citation for an E-mail

❑ Begin by answering the question *Who wrote the information used?* The answer is the person who sent the email.

❑ The closest that an email comes to a title appears in the Subject line. Enclose it in quotation marks with a period. If there is nothing in the Subject line, go on to the next part of the citation.

❑ The descriptive phrase, "Message to _____." comes next. Fill in the blank with the name of the recipient or with the phrase "the author" if the student received the email.

❑ Add the complete date of the email.

❑ Finish with the medium of the source, "Email."

CITATION BASICS:

Examples:

Underwood, Jason. "X-rays." Message to the author. 5 June 2008. Email.

Jest, Shirley U. Message to Don Anderson. 26 Apr. 2007. Email.

Figure C.10. A citation for an e-mail.

Appendix D:
Examples of Citations for
Miscellaneous Sources

Citations for Recorded Music

- A citation for recorded music is very simple. It consists of the artist, the name of the recording, the label, and the date.

- Periods follow the artist and the recording, just as if the citation were for an author and his book.

- A comma separates the label and the date similar to the treatment of a publisher and copyright date.

- Only the unique name of the label is used. Do not include words such as *Recordings, Studio,* or *Records.*

- End with the medium of the source, such as "CD," "Audiocassette," or "LP."

CITATION BASICS:

- If a single selection on the CD is cited, it is included in quotation marks, just as if it were a selection within a book.
- If liner notes or a booklet is cited, start with its author and title, if they are available. Identify the medium as *Liner notes* or *Booklet.* Then give the citation for the recording.
- If the recording is accessed on the Internet, cite the artist, recording, Web site, sponsor, date, the designation *Web,* and the date of access.

Citations for Recorded Music

Springsteen, Bruce. *The Rising*. Columbia, 2002. CD.

This is a basic citation that includes the artist, the title of the CD, the record label, and the date of release.

Holly, Buddy. "It Doesn't Matter Anymore." By Paul Anka. *Buddy Holly: Greatest Hits*. MCA, 1995. CD.

This citation adds two elements: an individual song title (in quotations) and the writer of the song because the person is different from the recorder.

Garcia, Bob. Liner notes. *Joan Baez Greatest Hits*. By Joan Baez. A&M, 1996. CD.

This citation is for the untitled liner notes to a CD. If the liner notes were titled, the title would be included after the author and enclosed in quotation marks. The rest of the citation would be the same.

Figure D.1. Citations for recorded music.

Citations for Film

- Citations for film usually begin with the title of the film. It should be italicized because it is the title of a complete work, like a book, Web site, or sound recording.

- Follow the title with the name of the director, the distributor, and the date of release.

- The name of the director is preceded by the abbreviation *Dir.*, and the name is followed by a period.

- Only the unique name of the studio is used. Words such as *Studios, Company,* or *Productions* are not included in the citation.

- The name of the studio is followed by a comma, and the release date.

- End the citation with the medium used.

CITATION BASICS:

- End the citation with "Film" if the researcher attended a viewing of the work. Use other descriptors, as appropriate, such as DVD, Film-strip, or Slide program.

- If the film was viewed on television, use a citation for a television program.

- It is permissible to include additional information, such as the names of performers. These are preceded by the abbreviation *Perf.*

- Occasionally the writer is focusing on the work of an individual connected to a film, usually the director. In this case, the citation begins with that person's name followed by the appropriate abbreviation.

Citations for Film

Mystic River. Dir. Clint Eastwood. Warner Home Video, 2003. DVD.

This is a basic citation for a film. It includes the title of the film, the director, the distributor, and the date of release. Look for this information at the bottom of the case in very small type.

Rain Man. Special edition. Dir. Barry Levinson. Perf. Dustin Hoffman and Tom Cruise 1988. MGM Home Entertainment, 2004. DVD.

This citation contains three additional pieces of information: the fact that this release is a special edition, its two stars, and the original release date of the film, 1988. This particular DVD is a special edition, which is important to note in the citation because it helps the reader find the same release. The original release date of the film is included, as are the performers, because the writer is studying Oscar-winning films of the 1980s.

Hanks, Tom, perf. *Forrest Gump.* Dir. Robert Zemeckis. Paramount, 1994. Videocassette.

This citation begins with the name of the actor who portrays the title character because the researcher is writing a comparison/contrast paper on the characters portrayed by Tom Hanks.

Ford, John, dir. *The Grapes of Wrath.* Twentieth Century-Fox, 1967. Video-cassette.

This citation begins with the name of the director because the writer is studying the films directed by John Ford.

Figure D.2. Citations for film.

Citations for Works of Art

- Works of art most commonly include paintings, sculptures, and photographs.

- Works of art are very simple to cite. Begin with the name of the artist.

- Italicize the title of the piece.

- Next comes the date. If not known, use *N.d.*

- Next include the medium, e.g. painting, sculpture, photograph. (If appropriate, students may use a more descriptive phrase, such as "watercolor on canvas.")

- Include the name of the museum or other location that houses the piece, followed by a comma and the name of the city.

CITATION BASICS:

- If the writer is citing a picture of a piece of art, such as an illustration in an art book, then cite the book. Make sure to include the page or plate number. End the citation with the correct medium, *Print*.

- If the writer is citing a picture of a piece of art viewed on the Internet, it is only necessary to cite the Web site.

- A citation for a personal photograph begins with a brief description, e.g. "Statue of Liberty." Identify it as *Personal photograph of (the name of the person who took the picture)*. End with the date the photo was taken, written in the style of dates of periodicals and Web sites.

Citations for Works of Art

Evans, Walker. *Stable, Natchez, Mississippi*. 1935. Photograph. Metropolitan
Museum of Art, New York.

Here is a basic citation for a work of art. The citation begins with the artist, followed by the title of the piece, date, medium, and the location. This citation is
only correct if the writer is citing the actual piece. In other words, has the writer
viewed the piece in the Metropolitan Museum of Art in New York?

If the writer is using a photograph of the piece that appears in an art book, then
a citation for the book is sufficient. Delete the medium designation of the artwork and use the *Print* designation for the book at the end of the citation.

Evans, Walker. "Stable, Natchez, Mississippi." *Photography of the Depression*.
Ed. John Fields. Chicago: ArtWorld, 1996. Plate 352. Print.

If the piece were viewed on the Internet, then the citation would look as
follows:

Evans, Walker. "Stable, Natchez, Mississippi." *The Metropolitan Museum of
Art*. Metropolitan Museum of Art, 2009. Web. 12 April 2009.

Notice that the designation of *Photograph* is missing in this citation as well.
After the artist and the title of the piece, list the title of the Web site, the sponsor,
and date. Next comes the designation of *Web,* and the date the Web site was
accessed.

Empire State Building, New York. Personal photograph by author. 12 Sept.
2008.

If the writer is using a personal photograph taken by himself or someone else,
the citation should begin with a brief description of the subject of the photograph followed by the phrase *Personal photograph by* and the name of the photographer or the phrase *the author.* End with the date of the picture.

Figure D.3. Citations for works of art.

Citations for Television and Radio Programs

- Begin the citation for a radio or television program with the title of the segment in quotation marks. The title of the segment is not the name of the program. For example, the name of the program is *The Simpsons.* The title of the segment (or episode) might be "Bart Gets Expelled." This is similar to a chapter in a book or an article in a periodical. If the segment title is not broadcast, it may sometimes be found in published program listings. Sometimes it is not available.

- Italicize the title of the program.

- Follow the title of the program with the name of the network. The network may be local, such as ABC, NBC, or CBS, or it may be a cable channel, such as the History Channel or Disney.

- If the program was broadcast locally, include the call letters of the station and the city.

- Include the complete date of the broadcast.

- End the citation with the broadcast medium, either *Television* or *Radio.*

CITATION BASICS:

- As with many other miscellaneous sources, if the work of a particular individual is important to the writer, it is appropriate to begin the citation with that person's name.
- Other information can be included, such as narrator (Narr.), director (Dir.), performers (Perf.), and number of episodes.

Citations for Television and Radio Programs

"Japanese Balloon Bomb." *History Detectives*. PBS. WNTV, Greenville.
13 July 2008. Television.

This is a basic citation for an episode of a television program broadcast on a local channel.

Mariam McPartland's Piano Jazz. Natl. Public Radio. WEPR-FM, Greenville.
12 July 2008. Radio.

Charles, Ray, perf. *Mariam McPartland's Piano Jazz*. Natl. Public Radio. WEPR-
FM, Greenville. 12 July 2008. Radio.

The first citation for *Mariam McPartland's Piano Jazz* is a basic citation that lists the program (no segment title), the network, the local broadcast station, and the date the program aired. The second citation is for the same segment, but it begins with the name of the performer because it is important to the writer's work.

Figure D.4. Citations for television and radio programs.

Citations for Live Performances, Speeches, and Lectures

- Any live performance, such as a symphony, play, or concert, can be easily cited.

- Begin with the title, italicized.

- The next item is usually the author or composer, preceded by the word *By* and followed by a period.

- Include the name of the theater or other venue where the performance took place followed by the city. Separate these items by a comma.

- Include the date of the performance.

- End with the designation, "Performance."

CITATION BASICS:

- The names of performers and/or the director may be included between that of the author/composer and the name of the theater if the writer wishes to insert the information.

- As with the case of film, if the writer wishes to highlight the role of a specific individual, the citation may begin with the name of that person.

- Citations for speeches, lectures, and readings begin with the name of the speaker, the title of the address in quotation marks, the event, such as a conference, the sponsor, venue, the city, and the date.

- Identify the oration as a *Reading, Address, Speech,* or *Lecture.*

Citations for Live Performances, Speeches, and Lectures

Madama Butterfly. By Giacomo Puccini. Newberry Opera House, Newberry.

> 22 Jan. 2008. Performance.

This is a basic citation for a live performance. It includes the title of the performance, its composer, the venue and city, and the date of the performance.

Piano Quartet in C Minor, Op. 60. By Johannes Brahms CSO Chamber Players.

> Memorial Hall, Cincinnati. 30 Jan. 2009. Performance.

This citation cites a live performance with basic information and includes the name of the performing group.

Martell, Allison, perf. *Our Town.* By Thorton Wilder. Longstreet Theater, Mil-

> waukee. 17 July 2008. Performance.

This citation mentions the performer first because the writer is critiquing her work on stage.

King, Carl. "The Art of Biographical Writing." College of Education Writing

> Symposium. Museum of Education, University of South Carolina.
> 15 Mar. 2006. Lecture.

Be sure to add the proper type of description to the citation, such as speech, lecture, reading, or address. The program for the event should help.

Figure D.5. Citations for live performances, speeches, and lectures.

Citations for Interviews

❑ Citations for interviews are determined by the medium in which the interview appears. For example, an interview might be broadcast on television or radio, it may appear in print, it may be on the Internet, or it may even be conducted by the writer. If the writer is the interviewer, the interview takes place face-to-face (personal) or by telephone.

❑ Begin the citation with the name of the person who was interviewed.

❑ If the interview has a title, it should be enclosed in quotation marks as is the title of a television program or magazine article. If a title is not available, use the designation, *Interview.*

❑ If the interview was broadcast on television or radio, the citation should include the elements for a broadcast. End the citation with the designation *Television* or *Radio.*

❑ If the interview was published, the citation should include the elements for a book or periodical citation. End the citation with the designation *Print.*

❑ If the interview appeared on the Internet, follow the title of the interview (in quotation marks) with the name of the Web site (italicized). Follow with the sponsor, date of interview, the designation *Web* and the date of access.

❑ If the interview was conducted by the writer, it should be identified as a *Personal interview* (face-to-face) or *Telephone interview* and conclude with the date of the interview.

CITATION BASICS:

• The name of the interviewer can be included by using *Interview by* _____ .

Citations for Interviews

Walsh, Peter. "Walsh Plans a Busy Year Decluttering Homes, Lives." *Greenville News* 3 Jan. 2009, 6D. Print.

This is a basic citation for an interview of Peter Walsh that was published in a newspaper.

Clinton, Hillary. Interview. *In the News.* CNN. 4 Apr. 2009. Television.

This interview aired on television. The citation begins with the name of the person interviewed. There was no title for an episode, so the word *Interview* is included. The title of the program is in italics. The citation follows the format for a television program with the network coming next. No station and city are listed because it is a cable network, not a local one. Next comes the broadcast date, and the medium designation.

Greene, Maxine. "Maxine Greene: The Importance of Personal Reflection." *Edutopia.* George Lucas Educational Foundation, 2008. Web. 3 Jan. 2009.

This is an interview on the Web site of *Edutopia* magazine. The citation starts with the person interviewed. The title of the article and the name of the online periodical are followed by the sponsor, date, designation of medium, and date of access.

If the writer himself conducts the interviews, they are cited as follows:

Obama, Barack. Personal interview. 20 Jan. 2009.

Obama, Barack. Telephone interview. 20 Jan. 2009.

Figure D.6. Citations for interviews.

Appendix E: Works Cited Templates

Thanks to Lawren Hammond, formerly of North Augusta High School (South Carolina), for allowing me to use her student handout for citation formatting. The handout is the basis for the templates in this section. They should be useful for helping students get started or as a quick review.

WORKS CITED TEMPLATE

Books by One Author

Author (look on the Title Page) LastName, FirstName, MiddleName/Initial   .
Title of the Book (put a **:** between the title and the subtitle; italicize all of it)   .
City of Publication (look at the bottom of the title page—use the first city listed)   **:**
Publisher (just the name, not words like *Publishing, Press,* or *Company*)   **,**
Copyright Date (this is just a year and is on the back of the Title Page)   .
Pages (if you used only certain page numbers, put them last with a hyphen between the first and last and no *p.*) -   .   **Print.**

Now copy the citation information on the lines below. Be sure to:

- Put the information in the proper order.

- Include all the punctuation marks. Make sure to finish with "Print."

- Keep writing until you run out of room. Then go to the next line.

_____

_____

_____

_____

Figure E.1. Works cited template: Books by one author.

WORKS CITED TEMPLATE

Books by Two Authors

First Author
(look on the Title Page)
LastName, FirstName, MiddleName/Initial

, and

Second Author
(FirstName MiddleName/Initial LastName)

.

Title of the Book
(put a **:** between the title and the subtitle—italicize all of it)

.

City of Publication
(look at the bottom of the title page—use the first city listed)

:

Publisher
(just the name, not words like *Publishing, Press,* or *Company*)

,

Copyright Date
(this is just a year and is on the back of the Title Page)

.

Pages
(if you used only certain page numbers, put them last with a hyphen between the first and last and no *p.*)

- .

Print.

Now copy the citation information on the lines below. Be sure to:

- Keep writing on the lines until you come to the end. Then go to the next line.

- Include all the punctuation marks. Make sure to finish with "Print."

_____

_____

_____

Figure E.2. Works cited template: Books by two authors.

WORKS CITED TEMPLATE

Books by Three Authors

First Author
(look on the Title Page)
LastName, FirstName, MiddleName/Initial

,

Second Author
(FirstName MiddleName/Initial LastName)

, and

Third Author
(FirstName MiddleName/Initial LastName)

.

Title of the Book
(put a : between the title and the subtitle—italicize all of it)

.

City of Publication
(look at the bottom of the title page—use the first city listed)

:

Publisher
(just the name, not words like *Publishing, Press,* or *Company*)

,

Copyright Date
(this is just a year and is on the back of the Title Page)

.

Pages
(if you used only certain page numbers, put them last with a hyphen between the first and last and no *p*.)

-   .   **Print.**

Now copy the citation information on the lines below. Be sure to:

- Keep writing on the lines until you come to the end. Then go to the next line.

- Include all the punctuation marks. Make sure to finish with "Print."

_____

_____

_____

Figure E.3. Works cited template: Books by three authors.

WORKS CITED TEMPLATE

Books with a Subtitle

Author (look on the Title Page) LastName, FirstName, MiddleName/Initial <div align="right">.</div>
Title of the Book (put a : between the title and the subtitle—italicize all of it) <div align="right">:</div>
Subtitle of the Book (if there is one, it is usually beneath the title in smaller print) <div align="right">.</div>
City of Publication (look at the bottom of the Title Page—use the first city listed) <div align="right">:</div>
Publisher (just the name, not words like *Publishing, Press,* or *Company*) <div align="right">,</div>
Copyright Date (this is just a year and is on the back of the Title Page) <div align="right">.</div>
Pages (if you used only certain page numbers, put them last with a hyphen between the first and last and no *p.*) -   .   **Print.**

Now copy the citation information on the lines below. Be sure to:

- Keep writing on the lines until you come to the end. Then go to the next line.

- Include all the punctuation marks. Make sure to finish with "Print."

_____

_____

_____

Figure E.4. Works cited template: Books with a subtitle.

Book as an Edition

Author (look on the Title Page) LastName, FirstName, MiddleName/Initial •
Title of the Book (put a **:** between the title and the subtitle—italicize all of it) •
Edition of the Book (if there is one, it is usually beneath the title in smaller print) Rev. ed. or 2nd ed., for example •
City of Publication (look at the bottom of the Title Page—use the first city listed) :
Publisher (just the name, not words like *Publishing, Press,* or *Company*) ,
Copyright Date (this is just a year and is on the back of the Title Page) •
Pages (if you used only certain page numbers, put them last with a hyphen between the first and last and no *p.*)   -   •   **Print.**

Now copy the citation information on the lines below. Be sure to:

- Keep writing on the lines until you come to the end. Then go to the next line.

- Include all the punctuation marks. Make sure to finish with "Print."

_____

_____

_____

Figure E.5. Works cited template: Book as an edition.

WORKS CITED TEMPLATE

Books That Are Graphic Narratives

Author
(look on the Title Page)
LastName, FirstName, MiddleName/Initial

.

Title of the Book
(put a : between the title and the subtitle—italicize all of it)

.

Titles and Names of Other Collaborators
(list, in order, from the title page)

.

City of Publication
(look at the bottom of the Title Page—use the first city listed)

:

Publisher
(just the name, not words like *Publishing, Press,* or *Company*)

,

Copyright Date
(this is just a year and is on the back of the Title Page)

.

Pages
(if you used only certain page numbers, put them last with a hyphen between
the first and last and no *p.*)

-      .   **Print.**

Now copy the citation information on the lines below. Be sure to:

- Keep writing on the lines until you come to the end. Then go to the next line.

- Include all the punctuation marks. Make sure to finish with "Print."

_____

_____

_____

Figure E.6. Works cited template: Books that are graphic narratives.

Books with a Publisher's Imprint

Author (look on the Title Page) LastName, FirstName, MiddleName/Initial   .
Title of the Book (put a : between the title and the subtitle—italicize all of it)   .
City of Publication (look at the bottom of the title page—use the first city listed)   :
Publisher's Imprint (usually located above the publisher)   -
Publisher (just the name, not words like *Publishing, Press,* or *Company*)   *,*
Copyright Date (this is just a year and is on the back of the Title Page)   .
Pages (if you used only certain page numbers, put them last with a hyphen between the first and last and no *p.*)   -   .   **Print.**

Now copy the citation information on the lines below. Be sure to:

- Keep writing on the lines until you come to the end. Then go to the next line.

- Include all the punctuation marks. Make sure to finish with "Print."

_____

_____

_____

Figure E.7. Works cited template: Books with a publisher's imprint.

WORKS CITED TEMPLATE

Books with an Editor

Editor (look on the Title Page) LastName, FirstName, MiddleName/Initial	**, ed.**
Title of the Book (put a **:** between the title and the subtitle—italicize all of it)	•
City of Publication (look at the bottom of the Title Page—use the first city listed)	**:**
Publisher (just the name, not words like *Publishing, Press,* or *Company*)	**,**
Copyright Date (this is just a year and is on the back of the Title Page)	•
Pages (if you used only certain page numbers, put them last with a hyphen between the first and last and no *p.*) - •	**Print.**

Now copy the citation information on the lines below. Be sure to:

- Put the information in the proper order.

- Include all the punctuation marks. Make sure to finish with "Print."

- Keep writing until you run out of room. Then go to the next line.

_____

_____

_____

_____

Figure E.8. Works cited template: Books with an editor.

WORKS CITED TEMPLATE

Selection in an Edited Book

Author of chapter, article, or poem
(look in the Table of Contents) LastName, FirstName, MiddleName/Initial

.

Title of the Chapter, Article, or Poem
"   "
.

Title of the Book
(from the Title Page; make sure to italicize)

.

Editor of the Book
(this name is on the Title Page) FirstName MiddleName/Initial LastName
Ed.
.

Edition. Volume.
(if this information is on the Title Page, add it in the order given, each followed by a period)

City of Publication
(look at the bottom of the Title Page—use the first city listed)

:

Publisher
(just the name, not words like *Publishing*, *Press*, or *Company*)

,

Copyright Date
(this is just a year and is on the back of the Title Page)

.

Pages
(if you used only certain page numbers, put them last with a hyphen between
the first and last and no *p*.)

-          .   **Print.**

Now copy the citation information on the lines below. Be sure to:

- Keep writing on the lines until you come to the end. Then go to the next line.

- Include all the punctuation marks. Make sure to finish with "Print."

_____

_____

Figure E.9. Works cited template: Selection in an edited book.

WORKS CITED TEMPLATE

Two or More Selections in an Edited Book

Editor of the Book
(this name is on the Title Page) LastName, FirstName, MiddleName/Initial

, ed.

Title of the Book
(on the Title Page—italicize it)

.

Publication Information
(City: Publisher, Copyright Date.)

Print.

Now copy the citation information on the lines below.
Main Entry

_____

_____

Author of chapter, article, or poem
(in the Table of Contents) LastName, FirstName, MiddleName/Initial

.

Title of the Chapter, Article, or Poem
"   ."

Editor(s) (last name(s) only)

Page Numbers of the Chapter, Article, or Poem
(use a hyphen between the first and last # and no *p*.)

-         .

Now copy the citation information on the lines below.
Cross-Reference

_____

_____

Figure E.10. Works cited template: Two or more selections in an edited book.
(Continued)

Author of chapter, article, or poem   (in the Table of Contents) LastName, FirstName, MiddleName/Initial   •
Title of the Chapter, Article, or Poem   "   "   •
Page Numbers of the Chapter, Article, or Poem   (use a hyphen between the first and last # and no *p*)   -   •

Now copy the citation information on the lines below.
Cross Reference

_____

_____

_____

Repeat for as many selections as you used from the book in the Main Entry. These citations are alphabetized with the rest of your citations on the Works Cited page.

If you used only one selection from the Main Entry, do not use this format. Use the worksheet for a Selection in an Edited Book.

Figure E.10. *(Continued)*

WORKS CITED TEMPLATE

Unsigned Article in a Multivolume Set

Title of the Article
"   ."

Title of the Book
(from the Title Page; make sure to italicize)
                                                                    .

Editor of the Book
(this name is on the title page) FirstName MiddleName/Initial LastName
Ed.   .

Edition
(if there is one on the Title Page)
                                                                    .

Volume Number
(do not use Roman numerals or write the number as a word—use Arabic numbers)
Vol.   .

City of Publication
(look at the bottom of the title page—use the first city listed)
                                                                    :

Publisher
(just the name, not words like *Publishing, Press,* or *Company*)
                                                                    ,

Copyright Date
(this is just a year and is on the back of the Title Page)
                                                                    .

Pages
(if you used only certain page numbers, put them last with a hyphen between
the first and last and no *p.* Do not use page numbers if the articles
in the book are in alphabetical order)
         -        .   **Print.**

Now copy the citation information on the lines below. Be sure to:

- Keep writing on the lines until you come to the end. Then go to the next line.

- Include all the punctuation marks. Make sure to finish with "Print."

_____

_____

Figure E.11. Works cited template: Unsigned article in a multivolume set.

WORKS CITED TEMPLATE

Signed Article in a Multivolume Set

Author of article
(look at the beginning or end of the article) LastName, FirstName, MiddleName/Initial

.

Title of the Article
"

."

Title of the Book
(from the Title Page; make sure to italicize)

.

Editor of the Book
(this name is on the Title Page) FirstName MiddleName/Initial LastName
Ed.

.

Edition
(if one is listed on the Title Page)

.

Volume Number
(do not use Roman numerals or spell out the number—use Arabic numbers)
Vol.

.

City of Publication
(look at the bottom of the title page—use the first city listed)

:

Publisher
(just the name, not words like *Publishing, Press,* or *Company*)

,

Copyright Date
(this is just a year and is on the back of the Title Page)

.

Pages
(if you used only certain page numbers, put them last with a hyphen between
the first and last and no *p*.)

-      .   **Print.**

Now copy the citation information on the lines below. Be sure to:

- Keep writing on the lines until you come to the end. Then go to the next line.
- Include all the punctuation marks. Make sure to finish with "Print."

_____

_____

Figure E.12. Works cited template: Signed article in a multivolume set.

WORKS CITED TEMPLATE

Titled Volume in a Multivolume Set

Author of Article or Volume
(look on the article or on the Title Page) LastName, FirstName, MiddleName/Initial

•

Title of the Article
(if using the entire volume, skip this)

"   ."

Title of the Volume
(taken from the Title Page and italicized)

•

Editor
(if one is indicated on the Title Page)

•

Edition
(if one is indicated on the Title Page)

•

City of Publication
(look at the bottom of the Title Page—use the first city listed)

:

Publisher
(just the name, not words like *Publishing*, *Press*, or *Company*)

,

Copyright Date
(this is just a year and is on the back of the Title Page)

•

Pages (if you used only certain page numbers, put them last with
a hyphen between the first and last and no *p*.)

-        •
Print.

Supplementary Information
(although not required, it is acceptable to add the title of the multivolume set)
Italicize the title of the set.
Vol.   of   •

Now copy the citation information on the lines below. Be sure to:

- Keep writing on the lines until you come to the end. Then go to the next line.
- Include all the punctuation marks. Make sure to finish with "Print."

_____

_____

Figure E.13. Works cited template: Titled volume in a multivolume set.   *163*

WORKS CITED TEMPLATE

Encyclopedia Articles (Signed and Unsigned)

Author
(of the article, if there is one—look at the end of the article; it will be in small type)
LastName, FirstName, MiddleName/Initial

.

Title of the Article
(exactly as it appears)

"   "
.

Title of the encyclopedia
(italicized)

.

Date
(of the edition—look on the title page or cover)

ed. Print.

Now copy the citation information on the lines below. Be sure to:

- Put the information in the proper order.

- Start with the title of the article if there is no author given.

- Include all the punctuation marks. Make sure to finish with "Print."

- Keep writing until you run out of room on the line. Then go to the next line.

_____

_____

_____

_____

_____

Figure E.14. Works cited template: Encyclopedia articles (signed and unsigned).

WORKS CITED TEMPLATE

Magazine Articles

Author
(look at the beginning or the end of the article)
LastName, FirstName, MiddleName/Initial

.

Title of the Article
(exactly as it appears)

"   ."

Name of the Magazine
(italicized)

Date
(of the magazine—if it is weekly, write it DayMonthYear;
if it is monthly, write it MonthYear.)

:

Page Numbers
(if the article is complete on continuous pages,
use a hyphen, as in 56-62; if not, use a + as in 43+)

-        .   **Print.**

Now copy the citation information on the lines below. Be sure to:

- Put the information in the proper order.

- Start with the title of the article if there is no author given.

- Include all the punctuation marks. Make sure to finish with "Print."

- Keep writing until you run out of room on the line. Then go to the next line.

_____

_____

_____

Figure E.15. Works cited template: Magazine articles.

WORKS CITED TEMPLATE

Journal Articles

Author (look at the beginning or the end of the article) LastName, FirstName, MiddleName/Initial .
Title of the Article (exactly as it appears) ``   .''
Name of the Journal (italicized—if the title begins with the word *the,* omit it)
Volume, Issue, and Year of the journal—volume.issue (year): .   (   ):
Page Numbers (if the article is complete on continuous pages, use a hyphen, as in 56-62; if not, use a + as in 43+) –   .   **Print.**

Now copy the citation information on the lines below. Be sure to:

- Put the information in the proper order.
- Start with the title of the article if there is no author given.
- Include all the punctuation marks. Make sure to finish with "Print."
- Keep writing until you run out of room on the line. Then go to the next line.

_____

_____

_____

_____

Figure E.16. Works cited template: Journal articles.

WORKS CITED TEMPLATE

Newspaper Articles

Author (look at the beginning of the article) LastName, FirstName, MiddleName/Initial   .
Title of the Article (exactly as it appears) "   .""
Name of the Newspaper (italicized—if the title begins with *The,* omit it; if it does not include the location, put it after the title in brackets [   ])
Date (of the newspaper. Look on the masthead. Write the date as Day Month Year.)   ,
Edition (of the newspaper. Look on the masthead.)   **ed.:**
Page Numbers (if the article is complete on continuous pages, use a hyphen, as in 56-62; if not, use a + as in 43+)   -   .   **Print.**

Now copy the citation information on the lines below. Be sure to:

- Put the information in the proper order.

- Start with the title of the article if there is no author given.

- Include all the punctuation marks. Make sure to finish with "Print."

- Keep writing until you run out of room on the line. Then go to the next line.

_____

_____

_____

Figure E.17. Works cited template: Newspaper articles.

WORKS CITED TEMPLATE

Online Encyclopedia Article

Name of the Author (if there is one given; LastName, FirstName, MiddleName/Initial) .
Title of the Article ``   '' .
Title of the Encyclopedia (look at the top of the home page; italicize) .
Publisher or Sponsor (on the home page, if there is one—if none given, use *N.p.*) ,
Date of Publication (or date of latest update; Day Month Year—if not date use *n.d.*) .
Designation of Medium **Web.**
Date of Access (when you visited the site; Day Month Year) .

Now copy the citation information on the lines below. Be sure to:

- Put the information in the proper order.

- Keep writing on a line until you run out of room.

- Include all the punctuation marks.

_____

_____

_____

Figure E.18. Works cited template: Online encyclopedia article.

WORKS CITED TEMPLATE

Web Page

Name of the Author (if there is one given; LastName, FirstName, MiddleName/Initial) •
Title of the Web Page "   ". "
Title of the Web Site (look at the top of the home page; italicized) •
Publisher or Sponsor (on the home page, if there is one—if none given, use *N.p.*) ,
Date of Publication (or date of latest update; Day Month Year—if no date, use *n.d.*) •
Designation of Medium **Web.**
Date of Access (when you visited the site; Day Month Year) •

Now copy the citation information on the lines below. Be sure to:

- Put the information in the proper order.

- Keep writing on a line until you run out of room.

- Include all the punctuation marks.

_____

_____

_____

Figure E.19. Works cited template: Web page.

WORKS CITED TEMPLATE

Web Site

Author of the Web Site (if one is given, LastName, FirstName, MiddleInitial/Name)   .
Name of the Web Site (look at the top of the home page; italicize)   .
Publisher or Sponsor (on the home page, if there is one—if none given use *N.p.*)   ,
Date of Publication (or date of latest update; Day Month Year—if none given use *n.d.*)   .
Designation of Medium   **Web.**
Date of Access (when you visited the site; Day Month Year)   .

Now copy the citation information on the lines below. Be sure to:

- Put the information in the proper order.

- Keep writing on a line until you run out of room.

- Include all the punctuation marks.

_____

_____

_____

_____

Figure E.20. Works cited template: Web site.

WORKS CITED TEMPLATE

Article on a Wiki

Title of the Article (exactly as it appears) "⟨⟩."
Name of Wiki (look at the top of the home page; italicized) .
Publisher or Sponsor (on the home page, if there is one—if none given, use *N.p.*) ,
Date of Posting (Day Month Year—if none given use *n.d.*) .
Designation of Medium   **Web.**
Date of Access (when you visited the site; Day Month Year) .

Now copy the citation information on the lines below. Be sure to:

- Put the information in the proper order.

- Keep writing until you run out of room. Then go to the next line.

- Include all the punctuation marks.

_____

_____

_____

_____

Figure E.21. Works cited template: Article on a wiki.

WORKS CITED TEMPLATE

Blog or Discussion Board Entry

Author
(if there is one; if not, begin with the title of the article)
LastName, FirstName, MiddleName/Initial

.

Title of the Blog or Discussion Board Entry
(exactly as it appears)

" "
.

Title of the Web Site
(if there is one, use italics)

.

Publisher or Sponsor
(if there is none, then use *N.p.*)

,

Date of Posting
(Day Month Year)

.

Designation of Medium

Web.

Date of Access
(when you visited the site; Day Month Year)

.

Now copy the citation information on the lines below. Be sure to:

- Put the information in the proper order.

- Keep writing until you run out of room. Then go to the next line.

- Include all the punctuation marks.

_____

_____

_____

Figure E.22. Works cited template: Blog or discussion board entry.

WORKS CITED TEMPLATE

Article in an Online Periodical

Name of the Author
(if there is one given; LastName, FirstName, MiddleName/Initial)

.

Title of the Article

"   *"*
.

Name of the Periodical
(look at the top of the home page; italicize)

.

Publisher or Sponsor
(if given—if none available, use *N.p.*)

,

Date of Publication
(or date of latest update; Day Month Year—if none given, use *n.d.*)

.

Designation of Medium

Web.

Date of Access
(when you visited the site; Day Month Year)

.

Now copy the citation information on the lines below. Be sure to:

- Put the information in the proper order.

- Keep writing on a line until you run out of room.

- Include all the punctuation marks.

_____

_____

_____

Figure E.23. Works cited template: Article in an online periodical.

WORKS CITED TEMPLATE

Nonprint Material on the Web

Name of the Author or Artist (if there is one given; LastName, FirstName, MiddleName/Initial) •
Title of the Work "   " •
Title of the Web Site (look at the top of the home page; italicized) •
Edition or Version (if given) •
Person Who Posted the Material (if different than the author or artist) •
Publisher or Sponsor (on the home page, if there is one—if none given, use *N.p.*) ,
Date of Publication (or date of latest update; Day Month Year—if no date, use *n.d.*) •
Designation of Medium   **Web.**
Date of Access (when you visited the site; Day Month Year) •

Now copy the citation information on the lines below. Be sure to:

- Put the information in the proper order.

- Keep writing on a line until you run out of room.

- Include all the punctuation marks.

_____

_____

Figure E.24. Works cited template: Nonprint material on the Web.

WORKS CITED TEMPLATE

Article in an Online Scholarly Journal

Name of the Author
(if there is one given; LastName, FirstName, MiddleName/Initial)

.

Title of the Article

" *."*

Name of the Journal
(look at the top of the home page; italicize)

Volume, Issue, and Year
(written as vol.issue(year) or vol(year))

:

Pages
(if page numbers are given, use them; if not, use *n. pag.*)

n. pag.

Designation of Medium

Web.

Date of Access
(when you visited the site; Day Month Year)

.

Now copy the citation information on the lines below. Be sure to:

- Put the information in the proper order.

- Keep writing on a line until you run out of room.

- Include all the punctuation marks.

_____

_____

_____

Figure E.25. Works cited template: Article in an online scholarly journal.

WORKS CITED TEMPLATE

Article in an Online Database

To cite an article in an online database, begin the citation as if you were using the print version of the article. In other words, if it is a newspaper article, use the template for newspaper articles. If it is a scholarly journal, use that template. Make sure to **delete** the original medium designation, *Print*. When the citation for the print version is complete, add the following information:

Name of Database   (italicized)   .
Designation of Medium   <div align="right">**Web.**</div>
Date of Access   (when you visited the site; Day Month Year)   .

Now copy the citation information on the lines below. Be sure to:

- Put the information in the proper order.

- Keep writing on a line until you run out of room.

- Include all the punctuation marks.

_____

_____

_____

_____

Figure E.26. Works cited template: Article in an online database.

WORKS CITED TEMPLATE

E-mail

Author
(the person who sent the e-mail)
LastName, FirstName, MiddleName/Initial

                        •

Title of the e-mail
(whatever appears in the Subject line, exactly as it appears)

"   ."

Name of the Recipient
(if the recipient is the student, use the words "the author")

E-mail to   •

Date
(of the e-mail. Write the date as Day Month Year)

                        •

Now copy the citation information on the lines below. Be sure to:

- Put the information in the proper order.

- Keep writing until you run out of room. Then go to the next line.

- Include all the punctuation marks.

_____

_____

_____

_____

Figure E.27. Works cited template: E-mail.

WORKS CITED TEMPLATE

Recorded Music

Name of the Recording Artist
(LastName, FirstName, MiddleName/Initial)

.

Title of the Song
(skip this if you are citing the entire CD)

"   ."

Writer of the Song
(skip this if you are citing the entire CD)

By   .

Title of the CD
(italicized)

.

Recording Label

,

Date of Release
(this date is only the year)

.

Recording Medium
(usually CD, but could be audiocassette or LP)

CD.

Now copy the citation information on the lines below. Be sure to:

- Put the information in the proper order.

- Keep writing on a line until you run out of room.

- Include all the punctuation marks. Be sure to include the recording medium.

_____

_____

_____

Figure E.28. Works cited template: Recorded music.

WORKS CITED TEMPLATE

Films

Name of the Director or Performer (start with a name if you are studying that person; LastName, FirstName, MiddleName/Initial, followed by the abbreviation dir. or perf.) ●
Title of the Film (start with the title if you are citing the film in general—italicized) ●
Name of the Director and/or Performers (if you did not begin the citation with the name of the director, include it here beginning with the abbreviation Dir. You may also include performers, beginning with Perf.) ●
Distributor of the DVD (usually in small type at the bottom of the case) ,
Date of Release (this date is only the year) ●
Film Medium (usually DVD, but could be videocassette, slide presentation, etc.) **DVD.**

Now copy the citation information on the lines below. Be sure to:

- Put the information in the proper order.

- Keep writing on a line until you run out of room.

- Include all the punctuation marks.

_____

_____

_____

_____

Figure E.29. Works cited template: Films.

WORKS CITED TEMPLATE

Works of Art

Name of the Artist   (LastName, FirstName, MiddleName/Initial)   •
Title of the Work of Art   (italicized)   •
Date of Composition   (year only)   •
Medium   •
Location of the Artwork   (museum and city) This is the end of the citation if the artwork was viewed in person.   , •

If the artwork was viewed as a reproduction in a book, delete the date of composition, medium, and location of the artwork unless instructed otherwise. After the title of the work of art, add the following information to the preceding template:

Title of Book   (if the artwork was viewed not in person but in a book,   that information must be included in the citation, italicized)   •
Author or Editor   (begin with the word By or Edited by)   •
Publication Information   (city: publisher, copyright date)   •
Page Numbers   (separated by a hyphen)   – •   **Print.**

Figure E.30. Works cited template: Works of art.

Now copy the citation information on the lines below. Be sure to:

- Put the information in the proper order.

- Keep writing on a line until you run out of room.

- Include all the punctuation marks. Make sure to finish with "Print."

_____

_____

_____

_____

Figure E.30. *(Continued)*

WORKS CITED TEMPLATE

Personal Photographs

Subject of the Photograph
(a name or brief description)

  •

Name of the Photographer
(if the author took the photograph, use the phrase *the author*)

Personal photograph by
  •

Date of the Photograph
(Day Month Year)

  •

Now copy the citation information on the lines below. Be sure to:

- Put the information in the proper order.

- Keep writing on a line until you run out of room.

- Include all the punctuation marks.

_____

_____

_____

_____

_____

Figure E.31. Works cited template: Personal photographs.

WORKS CITED TEMPLATE

Television and Radio Programs

Name of the Performer
(begin with a name only if you are studying that person; if not, begin with
the title of the episode. LastName, FirstName, MiddleName/Initial, perf)

                                                      •

Title of the Episode
(if it is available)

  "   ."

Title of the Program
(italicized)

                                                      •

Network

                                                      •

Local Broadcast Station and City
(separate the station and city with a comma; skip if not a local broadcast)

            ,   •

Broadcast Date
(Day Month Year)

                                                    •

Broadcast Medium
(Television or Radio)

                                                  •

Now copy the citation information on the lines below. Be sure to:

- Put the information in the proper order.

- Keep writing on a line until you run out of room.

- Include all the punctuation marks.

_____

_____

_____

Figure E.32. Works cited template: Television and radio programs.

WORKS CITED TEMPLATE

Live Performances: Symphony, Play, or Concert

Title of the Performance (italicized)   .
Author or Composer (FirstName MiddleName/Initial LastName) **By**   .
Name of the Performers or Musicians (if needed)   .
Venue and City (venue and city are separated by a comma)   ,   .
Date of the Performance (Day Month Year)   .
Medium   **Performance.**

Now copy the citation information on the lines below. Be sure to:

- Put the information in the proper order.

- Keep writing on a line until you run out of room.

- Include all the punctuation marks.

_____

_____

_____

_____

Figure E.33. Works cited template: Live performances: symphony, play, or concert.

WORKS CITED TEMPLATE

Live Performances: Lecture, Speech, or Reading

Name of the Speaker
(LastName, FirstName, MiddleInitial/Name)

•

Title of the Address
"   ."''

Title of the Author/Composer
(if different from the speaker, FirstName LastName)

By   •

Name of the Event
(conference, symposium, etc., usually found on a program)

•

Venue and City
(venue and city are separated by a comma)

,   •

Date of the Performance
(Day Month Year)

•

Medium Designation
(Speech, Lecture, Address, or Reading)

•

Now copy the citation information on the lines below. Be sure to:

- Put the information in the proper order.

- Keep writing on a line until you run out of room.

- Include all the punctuation marks.

_____

_____

_____

Figure E.34. Works cited template: Live performances: lecture, speech, or reading.

WORKS CITED TEMPLATE

Published Interviews

Name of the Person Interviewed (LastName, FirstName, MiddleName/Initial) ●
Title of the Article (If there is no title, use the word *Interview,* not italicized and without quotation marks) " ●."
Name of the Publication (italicized)
Date of Publication (use appropriate format for magazine, newspaper, or scholarly journal) ●
Page Numbers (separated with a hyphen if they are continuous; use the + symbol if not continuous) -   ●   ●
Designation of Medium **Print.**

Note: For interviews published on the Web or broadcast on television or radio, follow the format for those media after the person's name.

Now copy the citation information on the lines below. Be sure to:

- Put the information in the proper order.

- Keep writing on a line until you run out of room.

- Include all the punctuation marks.

_____

_____

_____

Figure E.35. Works cited template: Published interviews.

WORKS CITED TEMPLATE

Broadcast Interviews

Name of the Person Interviewed (LastName, FirstName, MiddleName/Initial)   .
Title of the Segment (if there is no title, use the phrase *Interview by* with the interviewer's name—no italics or quotes) "   ."
Name of the Program (italicized)   .
Network   .
Local Broadcast Station and City (separate the station and city with a comma; skip if not a local broadcast)   ,   .
Broadcast Date (Day Month Year)   .
Broadcast Medium (Television or Radio)   .

Now copy the citation information on the lines below. Be sure to:

- Put the information in the proper order.

- Keep writing on a line until you run out of room.

- Include all the punctuation marks.

_____

_____

_____

Figure E.36. Works cited template: Broadcast interviews.

WORKS CITED TEMPLATE

Student Interviews

Name of the Person Interviewed
(LastName, FirstName, MiddleName/Initial)

.

Interview Designation
(Personal or Telephone)

interview.

Date of Interview
(Day Month Year)

.

Now copy the citation information on the lines below. Be sure to:

- Put the information in the proper order.

- Keep writing on a line until you run out of room.

- Include all the punctuation marks.

_____

_____

_____

_____

_____

Figure E.37. Works cited template: Student interviews.

WORKS CITED TEMPLATE

Notes

Citation for Your Book, Periodical, Online Information, or Other Source

_____

_____

_____

Notes from Your Source

Summary   **Pages Used** _____

_____

_____

_____

Paraphrase   **Pages Used** _____

_____

_____

_____

Quote   **Pages Used** _____

_____

_____

_____

Figure E.38. Works cited template: Notes.

Appendix F:
Teaching Activities

FILL IN THE BLANKS

This activity is helpful to introduce citations to students and to help them identify the title page of a book.

1. Select approximately six books with very simple citation information (e.g., one author, no subtitle). These books will probably be fiction. It does not matter as long as they are as simple as possible.

2. Copy the sentences below on the board or reproduce them for the class.

3. Use a document projector or overhead transparencies to project a book's first page and ask students if they see the information they need to fill in the blanks. They will see the title, but probably not much else.

4. Then project the next page (the title page) of the book, and ask again if they can fill in the blanks. Now they can, with help, except for the copyright date.

5. Project the copyright page, and show them where it is in the book.

6. This activity should be repeated enough times so that everyone in the class knows the title page and can recognize the information on it. Finally, the teacher can project a title page and ask each student to fill in the blanks individually. Check for understanding.

   The name of the author is _____ .

   The title of the book is _____ .

   The city where the book is published is _____ .

   The publishing company is _____ .

   The copyright date is _____ .

The list of blanks can be edited to become progressively harder by adding books with subtitles, books with more than one author, edited books, and so on. The list can also be edited to fit the type of source the students are citing. In this way, the activity can be continued to introduce students to more complex citations, such as those for articles in online databases.

Note: To extend the activity at each level, show students how to arrange the information with the appropriate punctuation to make a citation. Practice as a class, and then let students try individually.

Figure F.1. Teaching activity: Fill in the blanks.

THE NAME GAME

This is a quick and easy game to play as an introduction or a refresher when students are learning how to format author names in MLA citations.

- The best example is to start with yourself. For instance, I would say, "My name is Marilyn Heath, and if I wrote a book the citation would begin with my name, 'Heath, Marilyn.'" (Make sure to say the comma and the period, as in "Heath comma Marilyn period.")

- Then point to a student, and have the student say how his or her person's name would be entered in a citation. If he gets it right, they get to point to another student. Do this three or four times or until you think they understand.

- Then add your middle initial, as in, "My name is Marilyn S. Heath, and if I wrote a book the citation would begin with my name, 'Heath, Marilyn S.'"

- Point to another student, who will follow your lead, and so forth.

- You can make this game as complex as you desire, adding more than one "author," surnames, titles, and so on.

Figure F.2. Teaching activity: The name game.

WHAT'S IN A NAME?

This activity is a good way for students to learn to arrange names in a citation as well as what information is included as part of a name and what is not. This activity can be done initially as a class and then in groups, pairs, or individually to practice.

1. Introduce students to the concept of the inverted author name in a citation.

2. Practice with a few easy names. Ask students to invert their own names. For good measure, have them say the "comma" and the "period."

3. Now ask them to do it again, but this time they should add their middle initial.

4. Ask if anyone in class has a suffix, such as "Jr." or "II." Discuss as a class the various ways this information might be handled in a citation. Is it necessary? Where would it be likely to go? Explain that the information is necessary because it is part of the person's name. Show them where the suffix goes in a citation.

5. Project the table on page 74 to show them that titles and degrees are not the same as suffixes and are not part of a person's name.

6. Practice with the list of names at the end of this exercise. Go around the room, vote by "thumbs up, thumbs down," standing up, sitting down, or whatever fun way the students like to participate.

7. When they have mastered the concept, have each student write a name as it would appear in a citation.

PRACTICE NAMES

Bart Simpson

Gary Paulsen

Vivian van Velde

Michael J. Fox

Sarah Michelle Gellar

Figure F.3. Teaching activity: What's in a name?

C. Thomas Howell

LL Cool J

Laurie Halse Anderson

E. R. Frank

Lon Chaney, Jr.

Senator John S. McCain III

Hank Williams, Jr.

Sister Elizabeth Ross

Fr. Nathan Selmer

Gerald Gaddings, Ph.D.

Rep. Charles J. Rayburn

Dr. Raymond S. Hastings, Sr.

President Barack Obama

Leonardo da Vinci

Leonardo DiCaprio

Avi

Leslie Van Duzer

Judge Thomas Smith Gray

James W. Styles, Attorney at Law

Note: All titles are omitted from citations, as are degrees. Only suffixes are included.

Figure F.3. *(Continued)*

BOOKS I WANT TO READ

This activity gives students practice at writing citations and at summarizing. It works at any level and with every student, even those who do not like to read. The idea is not that they will actually read the books (although it would be nice if they did). The idea is that they select and find books, write brief summaries of the books, and write citations for them. The teacher may want them to select books in their content area, but this really is not necessary to learn the skills.

1. Students should have an idea about the types of books they would like to read before they get to the media center. Not all of them will. Make sure they understand they do not have to read them. All of their choices do not have to be on the same topic.

2. Students should select and find three books that they would like to read.

3. They should read the inside flap and/or the back cover or the table of contents to get an idea of what the book is about.

4. They then summarize the book in two or three sentences on an index card.

5. They should put citation information on the back of the card. (It is okay if they cannot craft a citation on the spot as long as they know what information to take with them; they can format it later, when they can look at the guidelines.)

6. The students should write the summaries as polished paragraphs with the citation at the beginning to create an annotated bibliography.

Note: This activity should be adjusted according to the grade level and expertise of the students.

Figure F.4. Teaching activity: Books I want to read.

ALPHABET JUMBLE

This activity is a lot of fun. It can be as active as the teacher or the media specialist wants it to be. The idea is to help students with their alphabetizing skills so that they can generate a Works Cited page with citations in the correct order.

1. Make citation cards using the citations provided or ones that you create. (You can easily reproduce this page and cut them apart, tape them on index cards, and laminate them if you want them to last.)

2. Give a card, face down, to each student with instructions not to look until you say "Go."

3. At your word, students are to stand up and rearrange themselves in alphabetical order, according to the citation in their hand.

4. The first row that finishes correctly is the winner.

5. Shuffle the cards and do the exercise again.

Note: If it gets too noisy tell the students that only one person in the row can talk. Or no one can talk. For the grand finale, have all the students rearrange themselves in alphabetical order—with no talking!

CITATIONS

Stewart, Robert, with Clint Twist and Edward Horton. *Mysteries of History.* Washington, DC: National Geographic Society, 2003. Print

Freedman, Russell. *Give Me Liberty! The Story of the Declaration of Independence.* New York: Holiday, 2000. Print.

Christian, Rebecca. *Cooking the Spanish Way.* Rev. and exp. ed. Minneapolis: Lerner, 2002. Print.

Shone, Rob. *Volcanoes.* New York: Rosen Central-Rosen, 2007. Print.

Herter, Caroline, Laurie Frankel, and Laura Lovett. *Photocraft: Cool Things to Do with the Pictures You Love.* New York: Bulfinch, 2005. Print.

Schomp, Virginia. *World War I.* New York: Benchmark-Marshall Cavendish, 2004. Print.

Figure F.5. Teaching activity: Alphabet jumble. *(Continued)*

Gard, Carolyn. *Cool Careers without College for People Who Love to Sell Things.* New York: Rosen, 2006. Print.

Lazarus, Emma. "The New Colossus." *101 Great American Poems.* Ed. The American Poetry and Literacy Project. Mineola: Dover, 1998. 33. Print.

Scieszka, Jon, ed. *Guys Write for* Guys Read. New York: Viking, 2005. Print.

Krentz, Peter. "Thirty Tyrants." *World Book Encyclopedia.* 2008 ed. Print.

"Quetzal." *Compton's Encyclopedia.* 2005 ed. Print.

Baird, Julia. "The Savvy, Salty Political Saint." *Newsweek* 24 Dec. 2007: 54+. Print.

Barone, Jennifer. "Better Water." *Discover* May 2008: 31–32. Print.

Grady, Michael P., Kristine C. Helbling, and Dennis R. Lubeck. "Teacher Professionalism since *A Nation at Risk.*" *Phi Delta Kappan* 89 (2008): 603+. Print.

Smiles, Tracey. "Connecting Literacy and Learning through Collaborative Action Research." *Voices from the Middle* 15.4 (2008): 32–39. Print.

Davidson, Paul. "Dramatic Utility Bill Increase Expected." *Greenville News* 16 June 2008, final ed.: A1+. Print.

"US Says Polar Bears Are Threatened Species." *Wikinews.* Wikimedia, 14 May 2008. Web. 14 June 2008.

"Microwaves." *The Electromagnetic Spectrum.* Ed. Ruth Netting. NASA, 27 Mar 2007. Web. 18 June 2008.

"Uncle Tom's Cabin and American Culture." *MSN Encarta.* Microsoft, 2008. Web. 14 June 2008.

Bruno. "Three Words That Could Overthrow Physics: 'What Is Magnetism?'" *Discover* 24 April 2008. n. pag. Web. 12 May 2008.

Figure F.5. *(Continued)*

Copeland, Larry. "Distractions Challenge Teen Drivers." *USA Today* 25 Jan. 2007. n. pag. *SIRS Knowledge Source.* Web. 5 Oct. 2007

Holly, Buddy. "It Doesn't Matter Anymore." By Paul Anka. *Buddy Holly Greatest Hits.* MCA, 1995. CD.

Rain Man. Special edition. Dir. Barry Levinson. Perf. Dustin Hoffman and Tom Cruise. 1988. MGM Home Entertainment, 2004. DVD.

Mariam McPartland's Piano Jazz. Natl. Public Radio. WEPR-FM, Greenville. 12 July 2008. Radio.

Charles, Ray, perf. *Mariam McPartland's Piano Jazz.* Natl. Public Radio. WEPR-FM, Greenville. 12 July 2008. Radio.

Madama Butterfly. By Giacomo Puccini. Newberry Opera House, Newberry. 22 Jan. 2008. Performance.

Piano Quartet in C Minor, Op. 60. By Johannes Brahms CSO Chamber Players. Memorial Hall, Cincinnati. 30 Jan. 2009. Performance.

Walsh, Peter. Interview. "Walsh Plans a Busy Year Decluttering Homes, Lives." *Greenville News* 3 Jan. 2009, 6D. Print.

Figure F.5. *(Continued)*

FAVORITES

This activity gives students practice in writing citations, using critical thinking skills, and persuasive writing. It works for any subject and every student.

1. Students should select their "favorite." It is up to the media specialist and the teacher to select the category. It can be a favorite sport, hobby, game, pet, author, genre, musician, artist, time in history, scientific discovery— just about anything.

2. During time in the media center, students are to find at least three facts from three different sources that support their choice. (It is a good idea to stick to print sources starting out, if possible.)

3. Students should write their facts on note cards and write the citation information on the back of the card.

4. Back in the classroom, they will create a persuasive paragraph using the information they gathered. They will also create a Works Cited page using their three sources.

Note: This activity can be adjusted to be easier or harder as necessary. For example, students could be required to find more sources, or they could be required to write a longer paper with parenthetical documentation as they become more adept. The idea is to introduce only one or two new concepts at a time, give them a chance to be successful, and give them plenty of practice.

Figure F.6. Teaching activity: Favorites.

WHAT AM I?

This is a typical matching activity. You can easily change it by inserting any of the citations from the Alphabet Jumble or ones that you or your students make.

1. Citation for a book by one author _____

2. Citation for a book by two authors _____

3. Citation for an encyclopedia _____

4. Citation for a newspaper article _____

5. Citation for a DVD _____

6. Citation for a book with an editor _____

7. Citation for a Web page _____

8. Citation for a subscription database _____

A. "Quetzal." *Compton's Encyclopedia.* 2005 ed. Print.

B. Hanks, Tom, perf. *Forrest Gump.* Dir. Robert Zemeckis. Paramount, 1994. Videocassette.

C. Copeland, Larry. "Distractions Challenge Teen Drivers." *USA Today* 25 Jan. 2007. N.p. *SIRS Knowledge Source.* Web. 5 Oct. 2007

D. "Microwaves." *The Electromagnetic Spectrum.* Ed. Ruth Netting. NASA, 27 Mar 2007. Web. 18 June 2008.

E. Bracken, Jeanne Munn, ed. *Women in the American Revolution.* Carlisle: Discovery, 1997. Print.

F. Davidson, Paul. "Dramatic Utility Bill Increase Expected." *Greenville News* 16 June 2008, final ed.: A1+. Print.

Figure F.7. Teaching activity: What am I? *(Continued)*

G. Myron, Vicki, with Bret Witter. *Dewey: The Small-Town Library Cat Who Touched the World.* New York: Grand Central, 2008. Print.

H. Giblin, James Cross. *The Life and Death of Adolf Hitler.* New York: Clarion, 2007. Print.

Note: For a real challenge, let them try to identify the citation without giving them choices.

Figure F.7. *(Continued)*

FIVE FAVORITE FACTS

Students often have a hard time learning how to summarize. "Putting it in their own words," as they are always told to do, is not as easy as we often think. Summarizing involves recognizing main ideas, supporting details, knowing synonyms, and being able to vary sentence structure. One way to give students practice is with short, easy-to-read nonfiction.

- Let students check out a short nonfiction book of their choosing. Just about any nonfiction will work, except some "how-to" books. A cookbook or drawing book, for example, would not be a good choice.

- Instruct students to skim their books, looking for "five favorite facts" as they read.

- By the time they have finished the book, they should have written a sentence stating each "favorite fact" and subsequent sentences explaining the fact (a short paragraph, but don't tell them that is what it is). The number of sentences depends upon the grade level of the students and how much summarizing practice they have had.

- Students should include a citation at the end of their facts, and each fact should include page numbers at the end as parenthetical documentation.

- Work with students as a class and then in small groups to help them modify their summaries as warranted.

- Soon they should be able to write five good summary paragraphs on any book they choose, and you will know they have mastered this important skill. They will also start to develop the habit of including parenthetical documentation and citations.

Figure F.8. Teaching activity: Five favorite facts.

COPY AND PASTE

This lesson on writing summaries was developed by Marsha Ratzel of Leawood Middle School (Kansas). It works well for those students who are glued to the computer. The objective is to have students write a two- to three-sentence summary of a short reading passage. Marsha was teaching computing, so she used the articles at the Intel Education Initiative Web site, http://www.intel.com/education/index.htm. Any short online articles selected to meet the abilities of your students will do.

- First, students copy and paste the entire article into a Word document.

- Then, after they read the article through, they read it again, using the highlighter to mark the main ideas in the article. They should mark words and phrases only—not complete sentences.

- Now they must look at the highlighted information and decide how they might relate the main points to compose their sentences.

- If they find that they have highlighted too much, they must go back and decide what is not a main point. Instead of undoing the highlight, they can use the strikethrough option; they might change their mind later.

- The students should write their final two- to three-sentence summaries at the bottom of the page in a different font color.

- Final summaries should be compared for the information they contain. Class discussion will help students understand the summarizing process.

- Length of articles and summaries should be adjusted according to student abilities.

Figure F.9. Teaching activity: Copy and paste.

SUM IT UP

This summarizing practice can be done with any short piece of text. An essential pre-activity is to make sure students know what summarizing is and that they have some whole class and/or group practice. Then, when you are certain that students are ready for more of a challenge, start them with a short piece of text—no more than a paragraph or two. Individually or in small groups, they should work on a summary.

After a short time, ask the groups to share their summaries. If possible, display two or three of them where the class can see them and compare them. Discuss the strengths of each and what makes each a good summary.

This activity can be done periodically whenever there is a little extra class time, with text that is increasingly longer and/or more complex.

Note: One way to add a little fun and interest is to use famous texts, such as the Pledge of Allegiance or the Gettysburg Address.

Figure F.10. Teaching activity: Sum it up.

IN A NUTSHELL

It is almost always a good idea to practice summarizing and paraphrasing before beginning any research project. Students can easily respond when asked what plagiarism is, but avoiding it while researching is another matter entirely. Summarizing and paraphrasing are not particularly easy skills to master; they take repeated practice because students must possess good reading skills, they must have rather extensive vocabularies, and they must be able to revise syntax.

A good way to begin building these skills is to practice taking notes from textbooks, lectures, and class discussions. A review of important main points can lead to writing good summaries and paraphrases. Practiced routinely, these two important writing skills—taking good notes and writing good summaries and paraphrases—will soon become familiar to students as they conduct research.

A good resource to introduce the topic is "Quoting, Paraphrasing, and Summarizing" at *The Owl at Purdue* Web site. The information at the site can easily be adjusted to the appropriate grade level. It does a good job of illustrating how the three techniques can work together for student writers. It also contains examples of well-paraphrased paragraphs and those that would be considered plagiarized. The Web address is http://owl.english.purdue.edu/owl/resource/563/01/.

Another good resource to teach paraphrasing is found at the Web site for the English Language Institute at http://oregonstate.edu/dept/eli/162paraphrase.html. This site includes Deborah Healey's four basic steps for writing a paraphrase, an example, and an online activity. Offline substitutes could easily be introduced to students who need easier material.

Finally, this six-page chapter gives teachers the basic information needed to teach summarizing and paraphrasing skills. It is clearly written, with pertinent examples. It is a great place to start for teachers who are themselves slightly uncertain about summarizing, paraphrasing, and plagiarism. This wonderful primer is found at http://www.landmarkoutreach.org/documents/SeditaSummarizing.pdf.

Figure F.11. Teaching activity: In a nutshell.

PRESEARCH BIBLIOGRAPHY

This activity is much like Books I Want to Read. It is a pre-research activity that will help students when they get to the real thing. It works in any content area and with every student. The goal of the activity is to help students "presearch" a topic they are interested in pursuing for their research assignment. It helps them practice skimming and scanning, note taking, and thinking critically about what they read. It also helps them settle on a manageable topic and formulate a research question.

1. Students should come to the media center with a topic already chosen. Once they begin searching the online catalog and databases, they will quickly discover if their topic is too broad or too narrow. The teacher and the media specialist should have already decided how to guide students toward workable topics.

2. Students should be instructed to select three to five sources that will help them with their research assignment.

3. Students then write a two- or three-sentence analysis of each source, paying special attention to the information that will be valuable to them. *Example: This database is more up-to-date than others I have found. The information on greenhouse gases is more detailed than what I need.*

4. They should write citation information on the back of each card.

5. This information will be valuable to them as they begin their research assignment and help them define their topic, as well as their research question.

Figure F.12. Teaching activity: Presearch bibliography.

Works Cited

Alexander, Lloyd. "The Truth about the World." *Guys Write for* Guys Read. Ed. Jon
Scieszka. New York: Viking, 2005. 13–14. Print.

American Association of School Librarians. *Standards for the 21st-Century Learner.*
American Library Association, 2009. Web. 27 Feb. 2009.

Berkowitz, Robert E., and Mike Eisenberg. *The Big6.* Big6, 2009. Web. 27 Feb. 2009.

Brizee, Allen, ed. "Quoting, Paraphrasing, and Summarizing." *The Owl at Purdue.*
Purdue University Online Writing Lab, 29 Apr. 2009. Web. 12 June 2009.

Buzzio, Toni. *Collaborating to Meet Standards: Teacher/Librarian Partnerships for
K-6.* 2nd ed. Worthington: Linworth, 2007. Print.

---. *Collaborating to Meet Standards: Teacher/Librarian Partnerships for K-2.*
Worthington: Linworth, 2007. Print.

---. *Collaborating to Meet Standards: Teacher/Librarian Partnerships for 7-12.*
Worthington: Linworth, 2002. Print.

Caspari, Ann K., Carol C. Kuhlthau, and Leslie K. Maniotes. *Guided Inquiry: Learning
in the 21st Century.* Santa Barbara: Libraries Unlimited, 2007. Print.

Dickinson, Emily. "There Is No Frigate Like a Book." *Poets.org.* Academy of American
Poets, 2009. Web. 12 June 2009.

Donham, Jean, et al. *Inquiry-Based Learning: Lessons from Library Power.* Worthington:
Linworth, 2001. Print.

Harada, Violet H., and Joan M. Yoshina. *Inquiry Learning through Librarian-Teacher
Partnerships.* Worthington: Linworth, 2004. Print.

Healey, Deborah. "ELI 162: Paraphrasing Steps and Examples." *The English Language
Institute.* Oregon State U, 9 Sept. 1999. Web. 12 June 2009.

Hollingsworth, Heather. "Colleges Sharpen Skills to Combat Cheating." *EssayInfo.com.*
Essay Writing Center, n.d. Web. 27 Feb. 2009.

"Killer Bib Tool." *Carmun.* Temair, 2008. Web. 11 June 2009.

"Knowledge Base." *NoodleTools.* NoodleTools, n.d. Web. 28 Feb. 2009.

Loertscher, David V. *Ban Those Bird Units! 15 Models for Teaching and Learning in
Information-Rich and Technology-Rich Environments.* Santa Barbara: Libraries
Unlimited, 2005. Print.

MLA Handbook for Writers of Research Papers. 7th ed. New York: MLA, 2009. Print.

"MLA." *NoodleBib Express.* NoodleTools, n.d. Web. 11 June 2009.

Modern Language Association. "Does the MLA Offer Software for Managing Citations?" *Frequently Asked Questions about the* MLA Handbook. MLA, 29 Apr. 2008. Web. 11 June 2009.

National Council of Teachers of English. *NCTE/IRA Standards for the English Language Arts.* NCTE, 2009. Web. 27 Feb. 2009.

Schrock, Kathy. *Kathy Schrock's Guide for Educators.* Discovery Education, 14 June 2009. Web. 14 June 2009.

Simpson, Carol. "Copyright and Plagiarism Guidelines for Students." *Carol Simpson, Ed.D., J.D.* N.p., n.d. Web. 12 June 2009.

Sizer, Theodore. *The Red Pencil: Convictions from Experience in Education.* New Haven: Yale UP, 2004. Print.

"Summarizing and Paraphrasing." *Landmark School Outreach Program.* Landmark Schools, Inc., 2008. Web. 12 June 2009.

Index